WORK'S
NEW AGE

DATE DUE

Oct 1, 2015	

PRINTED IN U.S.A.

WORK'S NEW AGE

The End of Full Employment
and
What It Means to You

James B. Huntington, Ph.D.

ROYAL
FLUSH
PRESS

Royal Flush Press
Eldred, New York

Royal Flush Press
P.O. Box 190
Eldred, NY 12732

orders@royalflushpress.com
www.royalflushpress.com

Edition ISBNs:
Softcover	978-0-9835006-3-6
PDF	978-0-9835006-4-3

Printed in the United States of America

Publisher's Cataloging-in-Publication
(Provided by Quality Books, Inc.)

Huntington, James B.
Work's new age: the end of full employment and what it means to you / James B. Huntington.
p. cm.
Includes bibliographical references and index.
LCCN 2011905514
ISBN-13: 978-0-9835006-3-6
ISBN-10: 0-9835006-3-0
ISBN-13: 978-0-9835006-4-3
ISBN-10: 0-9835006-4-9
1. Employment (Economic theory). 2. Economics—United States. 3. United States--Economic conditions.
I. Title.
HD5701.5.H86 2011
331.12
QBI11-600107

To Mary, my old friend and new bride

Work's New Age Principles

PRINCIPLE #1: Profitable and growing companies do not consistently add workers anymore.

PRINCIPLE #2: Major future inventions will have nowhere near the employment-boosting effect as cars, electricity, or television did in the past, as their work processes will be far too automated.

PRINCIPLE #3: Automation and scalability each damage the connection between work and consumption; their combination destroys it.

PRINCIPLE #4: Efficiencies discovered during bad times carry on to good times.

PRINCIPLE #5: Since adoption of retirement at age 65, American life expectancy has increased so much that if indexed in the same way now, retirement would be at age 98.

PRINCIPLE #6: Job ads no longer mean job hiring.

PRINCIPLE #7: America now has excess capacity—in workers.

PRINCIPLE #8: Younger people, especially those under 20, have become less and less likely to work at all.

PRINCIPLE #9: From the point of view of customers, trading one product for another is the same as taking the resources needed for the first and making the second with them instead.

PRINCIPLE #10: If American workers are too expensive on the world market, then comparative advantage theory says America should produce fewer workers.

PRINCIPLE #11: If ten million people go into business and half lose money, then only five million had the equivalent of jobs.

PRINCIPLE #12: Although America has no universal health care, its government all by itself paid more per person than those of eight other developed countries with coverage for all.

PRINCIPLE #13: In order for markets to work, people must have money to spend.

PRINCIPLE #14: One person earning $5 million per year does not spend as much on goods and services as 100 people earning $50,000 apiece.

PRINCIPLE #15: Factory jobs replaced farm jobs. Service jobs replaced factory jobs. No paid work that we know of now will replace service jobs.

Table of Contents

Table of Figures 11
Acknowledgments. 13

Introduction: A Shift for the Ages 15

Part I: The Problem
Chapter 1: Full Employment's End: Now and So Far 17
Chapter 2: It'll Get Worse. 43
Chapter 3: The Effects, So Far and Soon. 79

Part II: The Solutions
Chapter 4: What Do the Papers Say?. 99
Chapter 5: Non-Solutions. 103
Chapter 6: Partial Solutions. 117
Chapter 7: Valuable Possibilities 127
Chapter 8: Thinking the Not-So-Unthinkable:
    Guaranteed Income. 143

Part III: Action
Chapter 9: How Can We Adjust? Changing Our Lives
    and Our Heads 153

Postscript: Back to Us 159

Endnotes. 163
Index. 205
About the Author 217

Table of Figures

Figure 1:
Major Events Leading Up to Work's New Age 19

Figure 2:
Overall Labor Force Participation Rate, 1973–2010 20

Figure 3:
Major Events of Work's New Age 22

Figure 4:
Number Unemployed by Age, 1973–2010 24

Figure 5:
Unemployment Rate, Percent, 1973–2010 24

Figure 6:
Unemployment Rates by Age, Percent, 1973–2010. 25

Figure 7:
Median Weeks Unemployed, 1973–2010 25

Figure 8:
Number Unemployed for 27 Weeks or More, 1973–2010   26

Figure 9:
Mean Weeks Unemployed, and Percent of Jobless People
Unemployed for 27 Weeks or More, 1973–2010. 26

Figure 10:
Percentage of Labor Force with at Least a Four-Year
College Degree, 1990–2008 29

Figure 11:
The 15 Different Employment Statuses and Where They
Fit In. 33

Figure 12:
The 15 Employment Categories Plus Potential Immigrants,
with Total Numbers, Percentages, and Latent Demand
for Jobs 37

Figure 13:
Overall Model of Employment Status Movement—
More Jobs 38

Figure 14:
Overall Model of Employment Status Movement—
Fewer Jobs. 39

Figure 15:
Relationship Between Output and Amount of Labor Required,
by Number of Items Produced—Pre-Industrial. 53

Figure 16:
Relationship Between Output and Amount of Labor Required,
by Number of Items Produced—Industrial 54

Figure 17:
Relationship Between Output and Amount of Labor Required,
by Number of Items Produced—Post-Industrial 55

Figure 18:
Goods and Services by Automatability and Scalability. 57

Figure 19:
Productivity Indexes—Output, Output per Person,
and Employment. 64

Figure 20:
Number Participating in the Labor Force Aged 55+
by Age Group for 1986, 1996, and 2006, and Projected
for 2016 68

Figure 21:
Labor Force Participation Rate by Age, 1973–2010. 84

Figure 22:
Percent of People 55 and Older with Work Experience
during the Year by Age, 1987–2007 88

Figure 23:
Percentage in Labor Force by Sex, Ages 16+, 1970–2010 95

Figure 24:
Disposition of the 28 Employment-Boosting Suggestions . . . 102

Figure 25:
Minimum Wage in Current and Constant Dollars,
1973–2009 139

Figure 26:
Comparison of Guaranteed Income Systems 146

Figure 27:
Employment by Primary, Secondary, and Tertiary Work Sectors,
1961–2010 149

Acknowledgements

Chris DiNatale of DiNatale Design (www.dinataledesign.com) crafted and put the book cover together and designed the Royal Flush Press logo. Lars Clausen of American Author (www.americanauthor.com) provided the website and helped further with it. Editing and proofreading was by Mim Eisenberg of WordCraft (www.wordcraftservices.com), Jean Oplinger (jeanoplinger@gmail.com) completed the indexing, and Angela Werner (www.heyneon.com) designed and typeset the book. Printing was done by Color House Graphics (www.colorhousegraphics.com).

Thanks to Bill James for permission to reprint his passage on losing skills by not working.

Special thanks to those who came before me in perceiving the permanence of job losses, especially Jeremy Rifkin, Martin Ford, and Don Peck.

I thank my friends, relatives, and colleagues who served as an informal focus group on the book and provided other assistance: Sarah Chapin, Ping Chen, Jim Diederich, Diane Drey, Bill Evans, Ellen Faux, Sam Huntington, Skip Nelson, Mark Raphaelson, John Reitz, Tim Ricke, Diane Rozek, Jane Ann Scott, Sarah Yannett, Skip Yarian, and of course Mary.

Introduction: A Shift for the Ages

We must dare to prepare ourselves for the Exodus from 'work-based society': It no longer exists and will not return. —Andre Gorz[1]

Many of us have had the idea, in the back of our minds, that the number of people who want work will always roughly approximate the number of people needed for it. Classical economics assumes that free markets will always have many jobs.[2] Accordingly, when unemployment increases, it is due to bad times and will recover along with the economy. We have good reason to think that, because it has been correct since widespread work as we know it started with the Industrial Revolution. But, as the mutual funds always caution us, past performance does not guarantee future results.

This lifelong assumption we have is not true anymore. This is Work's New Age.

So what is the problem, how do we know it is permanent this time, and how can we solve it? This book seeks to answer those questions.

Part I: The Problem

Chapter 1

Full Employment's End: Now and So Far

Those who think some kind of robust recovery is hiding around the corner, just waiting to spring a pleasant surprise on us, are deluded.   —Bob Herbert[3]

On the Road to Work's New Age

Once upon a time, there was no unemployment. At least nobody called it that. Why? Because there were few jobs as we understand them today. As of 1800, about two-thirds of what would now be called working-class people had no steady income and survived through day labor, begging, and crime.[4] With the Industrial Revolution, the concept of employers' receiving set amounts of a worker's time in exchange for money became a social phenomenon.[5]

Before World War I, people without jobs were referred to as "idlers" or "loafers" instead of unemployed, as the latter suggested that people could be out of work because of others' choices.[6] Before 1914, instead of laying off some of their employees, companies were more likely to reduce hours across the board.[7] The Great Depression, still unmatched among American economic disasters, informed all of two things: The economy was interconnected, so the problems of people who lost their savings were not going to be limited to them, and even in the industrial world, there could be problems that would slash the number of jobs.

The country did not regain true prosperity before World War II, which filled up employment inside and outside the armed services. Afterwards, the greatest time of American affluence took hold. I call that era the "Winning by Default Years," since after that devastating conflict, the United States economy had no real competition. Economist Tyler Cowen in *The Great Stagnation*, describing America's pre-1975 ability to take advantage of relatively easy opportunities, had a similar idea.[8] As the baby boom generation started reaching working age, the country stayed out of recession, allowing it to absorb large gains in the labor force. Times were good, and expectations were high.

The seeds of coming employment problems, though, had been sown. In 1944, the G.I. Bill became law, and millions of servicemen and -women would use it to get the college educations many never thought they would have. In 1946, the first computer in the modern sense was produced. That had little immediate effect, but it started a chain of events which would lead to widespread automation. As college became routine in more and more American families, its graduates got a variety of good jobs, but a generation later their education began to outstrip the needs of the marketplace. During the 1960s, only 10% of those just finishing college took positions below their education level,[9] but that jumped up quickly, reaching 33% in 1970 and 1971,[10] caused at least in part by an increase in enrollment spurred by the Vietnam-era draft.

Figure 1 shows a timeline of the most important employment-related events leading up to the early 1970s.

It Arrived, But Was Hard to See

Economies in Europe and elsewhere had been getting more competitive with America's, but it was events in the Middle East

Year	Event	Why Significant
1787	First large American cotton mill[11]; Industrial Revolution in America started	Beginning of a vast number of jobs producing goods.
1929	Start of Great Depression	Ruined the economy. Personal failures much more severe than in recessions since, due to investments on margin.
1944	G.I. Bill signed into law	Foundation of college as the norm for smart middle-class high school graduates.
1945	End of World War II—start of Winning by Default Years	Twenty-eight-year era in which America had by far the largest economy, numerous industries had little or no presence elsewhere, and many jobs were available.
1946	ENIAC created[12]; first completely electronic programmable digital computer	Start of electronic work efficiency.
1961	Beginning of eight recession-free years	Minimized problems caused by the rapidly increasing number of labor force entrants.
1963	Concern about automation eliminating jobs reaches public eye[13]	Many people became aware of automation as a possible threat to employment and prosperity.
1964	First baby boomers turn 18	The number of people in the labor force began increasing substantially.
1969	ARPANET, forerunner of the Internet, starts operation	Beginning of communication between computers.
1970	Vietnam War—college enrollment increases	Many went to college to avoid combat, solidifying its status as the default choice after high school.

Figure 1: Major Events Leading Up to Work's New Age.

that caused the change. On August 23, 1973, in conjunction with the planned Yom Kippur War against Israel, the leaders of Saudi

Arabia and Egypt met and decided to manipulate the price and supply of oil as a weapon. From there, various Arab countries combined to create an oil embargo and forcibly imposed various price increases, which led to oil's per-barrel price quadrupling by the next year, ending at inflation-adjusted levels well above any time since the beginning of the automobile era.[14] The effect on Americans was strong, with industrial slowdowns, intermittent gasoline outages, the start of fuel rationing, and a recession. The situation would be resolved, but no more would unemployment maintain the levels of the 1960s.

Over the next few decades, job growth in non-recession years became smaller and smaller. During economic expansion times from 1950 through 1979, the number of non-government jobs increased an average of 3.5% per year. That dropped to 2.4% during similarly prosperous times from 1980 to 1999 and to 0.9% for the years of greatest growth in the 2000s.[15] Between December 1989 and December 1999 American payrolls grew by 21.7 million positions, but from December 1999 to December 2009 a net of 944,000 jobs was lost.[16] At the same time, more women went to work, and, as shown in Figure 2, the labor force increased in percentage, as well as in number, almost every year from 1973 to 1999.[17]

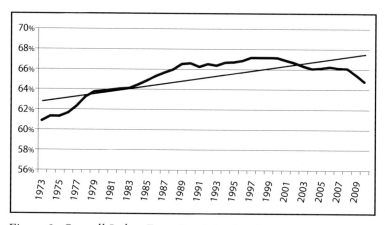

Figure 2: Overall Labor Force Participation Rate,
1973–2010 — 1947–1972 average: 59.3%

Other events set the stage for continued job losses. Mao Zedong's death and the invention of the World Wide Web led to China's vast exporting, connections between ordinary computers, and globalization as we know it today. Their effects on American jobs were concealed by the prosperity of the 1990s, the dot-com securities boom around 2000, and the real-estate-led consumer spending spree around 2005. Yet when housing prices returned to pre-2005 levels, the true situation became apparent. Figure 3 shows the most important happenings since 1973.

Much Clearer Now

Over the past 30 years, recovery after every recession has taken longer than it did for the one before,[21] with jobless ones now typical.[22] In 2009, when columnist and Nobel Prize-winning economist Paul Krugman said he had "no idea" how substantial and steady growth could resume, 44% of American families had at least one person whose pay was reduced, had their hours cut, or lost their job.[23] The 2000s became the first decade ever for median United States household income to decline.[24] The share of adult Americans working dropped from 63% to 58.4% from 2007 to 2010.[25] In August 2010 the number of jobs dropped in 42 states.[26] The number of positions needed to be added per month just to cover new labor force entrants was estimated from January 2010 and January 2011, by six different sources, as between 100,000 and 125,000,[27] and researcher Steven Blitz asked if large unemployment would persist indefinitely.[28]

As of May 2010, there were 8.4 million fewer jobs than at the former peak, 6 million of which may never return.[29] As of December 2010, 12 months after the recession's low point and 36 months after the all-time high in number of positions, 91% of the difference was still missing, making the 2008–2009 downturn not only the overwhelmingly deepest but by far the slowest recovering of any since 1970.[30] Many American companies increasing jobs in late 2010 were adding them in China, India, or other countries.[31] The mean February 2011 jobless time was 37.1 weeks.[32] In early 2010, surveys consistently showed that

Year	Event	Why Significant
1973	Oil crisis—end of Winning by Default Years	End of overwhelming American economic supremacy; start of Work's New Age.
1976	China's Mao Zedong dies—replaced by Deng Xaoping	Beginning of greatly expanded Chinese trade, which accelerated globalization.[18]
1978	Percent of women in labor force reaches 50%	Labor force increased greatly in relation to population.
1982	Last baby boomers turn 18	Effect of baby boom on labor force approached its peak.
1991	World Wide Web created	Beginning of connectivity crucial for globalization.[19]
1991	Beginning of nine recession-free years	Minimized problems of automation and globalization.
1995	Personal computers finally raise overall office productivity	Previously their effect on business efficiency was small, often nonexistent, but now they allowed office work to be done by fewer workers.
1999	Millennium Bug (Y2K) computer problem	Many Indian programmers solved it, showing that high-level outsourcing was viable.[20]
2005	Real estate boom; very high consumer spending	Masked problems of automation and globalization, as greater demand caused many jobs to be created.
2008	Real estate crisis; start of Great Recession	The price drop in personal homes, almost all bought effectively on margin, removed large money sources for many, and employment deflated.
2010	Recession over, but official unemployment goes above 10%, with all-time highs in number of jobless and average unemployment length	Economy reached a new normal state. The problems caused by Work's New Age were graphically revealed.

Figure 3: Major Events of Work's New Age

the economy was the foremost personal concern among Americans, with unemployment the component that required the most forceful, continuous, and comprehensive action; 52% in one poll named the economy or jobs as most important.[33]

Fifteen Different Employment Flavors

So there is less work than before, affecting those with and without jobs in different ways. As to personal relationships with employment, how many different formal statuses can people have? Some are easy: working, unemployed, and not wanting to work. Maybe you've heard of "discouraged jobless," for those who have given up looking, and of course there are people too disabled for employment. That's a good start, but those five make up fewer than half of those recognized by the U.S. Department of Labor, which has been creating and defining terms that have changed little or not at all since 1940.[34] All told, the Bureau of Labor Statistics (BLS) recognizes 11 general categories, to which I have added two from the U.S. Census Bureau, one outside normal population data, and one split out from another.

Unemployed

Officially unemployed people are those with no job, who looked for one in the previous four weeks (unless temporarily laid off and waiting for a call to return), and who are available to work. The unemployment rate is the number of unemployed people divided by the labor force, which is the sum of civilians employed and those officially unemployed.[35] Note that those who are not working and want to be may or may not be counted here.

Figures 4 through 9 show official unemployment trends since 1973. Figure 4 shows the total number of unemployed by age.[36] Figures 5 and 6 give overall rates and rates by age.[37] Figures 7 and 8 show the length of unemployment, expressed as the median number of weeks in Figure 7 and, in Figure 8, the number of people out of work for 27 weeks or more.[38] Figure 9 includes both mean weeks of unemployment and percent jobless for 27 weeks or longer.[39]

We can make several observations from these charts. In Figure 4, while the age composition of those unemployed has fluctuated

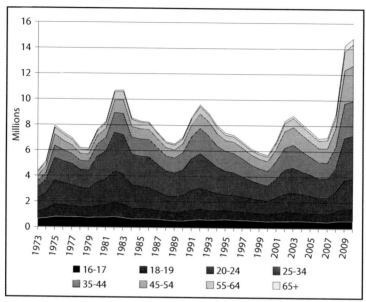

Figure 4: Number Unemployed by Age, 1973–2010
— 1948–1972 average total: 3.38 million

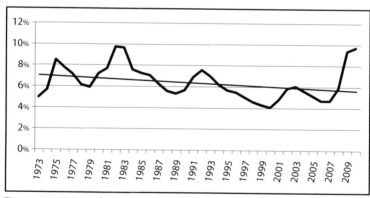

Figure 5: Unemployment Rate, Percent, 1973–2010
— 1947–1972 average: 4.74%

over time and has been affected by the ages of baby boomers, recent joblessness has been broad-based across age groups. Figure 5 shows a descending trend line over the 38 data collection years,

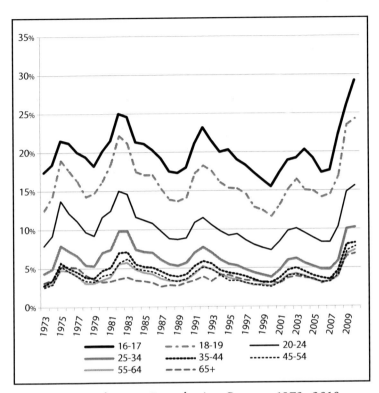

Figure 6: Unemployment Rates by Age, Percent, 1973–2010

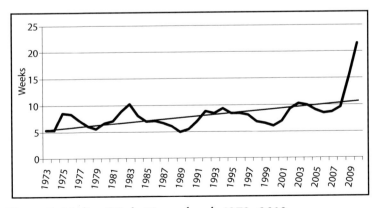

Figure 7: Median Weeks Unemployed, 1973–2010

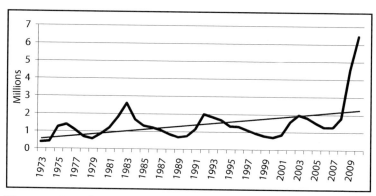

*Figure 8: Number Unemployed for 27 Weeks or More,
1973–2010 — 1948–1972 average: 346,000*

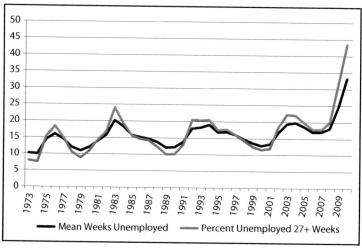

*Figure 9: Mean Weeks Unemployed, and Percent of Jobless People
Unemployed for 27 Weeks or More, 1973–2010 —
1948–1972 averages: 11.2 weeks and 9.5%*

a positive indicator but, as we will see, one with limited meaning. Figure 6 presents great differences between age groups under 35, with an almost perfect pattern of higher unemployment for those younger. In Figures 7 and 8, we see that unemployment durations have gone up and down with the economy, but with peaks and troughs both generally higher with time. Figure 9 shows that the percentage of those unemployed for 27 weeks or more is an exaggeration of higher mean jobless lengths; small increases in time without work go with big jumps in the share of those looking long.

Working Part-Time for Economic Reasons

Full-time work takes place when the employee usually puts in 35 hours or more per week, and part-time status applies for fewer. Those working part time for economic reasons, also called involuntary part time, include everyone working fewer than 35 weekly hours, saying they want to work full time, and available for the additional.[40] In 2003, the national average week for ordinary workers was 34 hours, the lowest since records were first kept in 1964.[41] By December 2009, it had fallen further to 33.2 hours,[42] but in November 2010 it was 34.3.[43] The 4.8 million working part time but wanting full-time employment in 2003 were the most in ten years,[44] and since then the number has gone much higher, to 5.9 million in 2008 and almost 8.9 million in 2010.[45]

Since part-timers as a group average about half time,[46] when considering the effect of involuntary part-time work on unemployment, it would be best to count each such worker as having half a job. For example, if of 100 million workers 10 million were jobless and 4 million worked part time for economic reasons, an unemployment rate of 12% would be more accurate than either the currently-presented 10% or a combination of 14%. However, the BLS, though it previously released a measure of unemployment treating involuntary part-time workers this way,[47] does not currently do that.

Underemployed Due to Money, Skill, or Values

Although "underemployment" is used in current economic reports to refer only to those working part time for economic reasons, historically it has had a broader meaning. In 1966, the International Labour Office said underemployment was the state "when a person's employment is inadequate, in relation to specified norms or alternative employment, account being taken of his occupational skill (training and work experience)." As the organization made clear, not only did part-time work when someone wanted full-time work (not enough hours) qualify as underemployment, but so did three other dimensions which considered the person's qualifications: not enough pay, not enough use of skills, and not enough productive values gained.[48]

Another term for underemployment has been "mismatch."[49] In 1969, 7.2% of the labor force was underemployed through low income, and 9.0% for skill or productivity mismatch. In 1973 the latter, which had worsened every year in between, reached 11.5%.[50] It continued to climb through the 1970s and included more than 14% of all workers by 1980.[51] By age, in 1969, 1975, and 1980, the shares of the labor force experiencing mismatch were averages of less than 1% for those 16 to 19, 13.3% of those 20 to 34, 11.8% of those 35 to 49, 8.9% of those 50 to 64, and 4.5% of workers 65 and older.[52] In a 1979 survey, more than 20% strongly disagreed that their positions facilitated use of their "skills and abilities."[53]

Underemployment in this broader sense, caused mostly by excess of supply over demand, reached significant levels among those with four-year college degrees in the 1970s.[54] The number of workers with degrees increased greatly from the 1960s through the 1980s.[55] As of 1975, almost 25% of all college graduates, not only recent ones, were working in positions below their educational knowledge,[56] and in 1976 one study concluded that schooling levels were outstripping those needed for the employment actually available.[57] Since then, as shown in Figure 10, the share of workers with college degrees has increased even more, and since 1990 has done so at a very consistent rate.[58]

The long-term effects of underemployment on careers go beyond immediate situations. In one study, college-educated people who lost suitable jobs and could find only mismatching ones had personal adjustment levels similar to those who were unemployed, and well below those with jobs at their educational

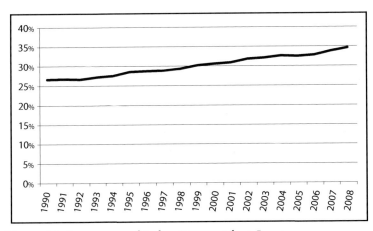

*Figure 10: Percentage of Labor Force with at Least
a Four-Year College Degree, 1990–2008*

standings.[59] Underemployment as of 1982 had become a stigma causing problems when applying for better positions, and professionally those underemployed suffered from skills deterioration similar to those jobless,[60] to be discussed later.

I estimate that 40% of all those working are underemployed by money, skill, or values. Some have considered the number much higher—I saw more than 60% in an early 1980s edition of Richard Bolles's jobseeking guide, *What Color Is Your Parachute?*. Although the BLS does not track underemployment in any form other than involuntary part-time work, it is real, important, and a growing characteristic of Work's New Age.

Solidly Employed

Employed people are all those who have worked at least one hour a week, had a job to which they did not report due to being sick or on vacation or for other such reasons, or worked at least 15 unpaid weekly hours for a family business.[61] The total working in America, peaking at 146 million in 2007, was 139 million in 2010.[62] All people with jobs, and not underemployed in any of the forms above, can be listed as solidly employed.

Discouraged

Discouraged workers are those without jobs, want them, are available for them, have searched for work within the past 12 months or sooner if after the end of their last position, and have stopped looking. They are considered "marginally attached" to the labor force.[63] Many are former job seekers now seeing insufficient hope to continue. The discouraged jobless often have low education and skills, positioning them poorly for recoveries.[64] There was an average of 1,173,000 people in this category in 2010, up from 369,000 in 2007.[65]

Family Responsibilities; In School or Training; Ill Health or Disability; Other

A substantial number of people are also counted as marginally attached but are not available to work. Their reasons for unavailability put them in any of four categories: unable to work because of family responsibilities; in school or receiving training; experiencing poor health or a disability; and an "other" grouping covering those with transportation, childcare, or undetermined issues.[66] These four included 1,026,000 people in 2007, and increased to 1,315,000 in 2010.[67]

Did Not Search for Work in Previous Year

These people say they want a job but have not looked for one for at least a year.[68] They are not differentiated further by the BLS and are not counted as marginally attached.[69] This category is much more populous than those just described, with 4,704,000 people in 2007 and 6,059,000 in 2010.[70]

Not Available to Work Now

These people have searched for work both within the last year and after their most recent job but are not currently available. They are not considered marginally attached.[71] There were 560,000 in this category in 2007 and 623,000 in 2010.[72]

Do Not Want a Job

Perhaps the easiest nonworking category to understand is those who are not only not available for a job but who do not want one. Most have consistently been age 55 or older[73] and numbered 74,041,000 in 2007 and 77,882,000 in 2010.[74]

Under Age 15 and Non-Civilian and Institutional Population 15+

Although the BLS does not provide labor data for those 15 years old, they are included in its civilian non-institutional population.[75] Accordingly, I have created two categories of American residents not counted previously. The first is the entire American resident population aged 0 to 14 from the U.S. Census Bureau, adjusted slightly to agree with their mid-2010 total population estimate of 309,050,816.[76] The second is the entire non-civilian and institutional population age 15 or higher, who are on active armed-forces duty or are institutionalized in such facilities as prisons, mental hospitals, or old-age homes,[77] determined by subtracting the total of all categories above from the 2010 population. The results are 62,142,928 aged 14 or less,[78] and 5,962,888 non-civilian or in institutions.

American Expatriates

The number of Americans living overseas has not been governmentally tabulated since 1999 and had not been regularly before then. By one approximation, as of 2006 about 3 million were moving to other countries each year. Estimates of the number of civilian United States citizens living elsewhere ranged from 4 million in an attempted 1999 government count[79] and just over 5 million appraised by the Association of Americans Resident Overseas in 2010[80] to a high-end 1999 guess of 7 million.[81] For this book, I have estimated 5 million American expatriates.

So how do these classifications fit together? Figure 11 shows the 15 different categories, whether they are counted in the census, how if at all they are included in the labor force, whether those in them are officially considered to want work, and if those in them have said they could take on a job.

Movement between employment statuses takes many different forms. In addition to discouraged workers, in 2009 approximately 1.6 million left the labor force to attend school or for other reasons.[82] Other recent choices among those not finding work have been retraining programs, family care, and, for recent college graduates, going to graduate school.[83] In addition, as of late 2010 more than 750,000 people were applying for Social Security disability every three months, more than one and a half times the 2006 number.[84]

The Hidden Reality: Latent Demand

Latent demand for jobs is a huge factor. While the BLS has many statistics such as most of those above, it is missing any indicator of how many people would apply for employment if they perceived there was a lot of it available.

In 2006, before the recession, a Wal-Mart opened just outside Chicago and advertised its 325 new jobs.[85] How many applicants did it get? More recent numbers show five or six jobseekers for each position, and at the time the Chicago area, with unemployment of 5.4%,[86] was much better off than that. Wal-Mart had received a lot of bad press earlier in the decade for its employment practices and work conditions—poor wages and few benefits were two of the major complaints—and in fact most of the 325 positions paid within a few hourly dollars of the minimum wage. Chicago, a large city, has education levels well above the national average, which means those jobs would not appeal at all to the bulk of those looking. So how many do you think applied for those 325 positions? A thousand? Two thousand? Five thousand, if that area of town was particularly bad off?

Not quite. The number of applicants for the 325 disparaged, low-paying, low-level, low-benefit, stereotypically undistinguished positions, during good economic times, at a company considered in many circles a notoriously bad employer, was… 25,000![87] How can you get an outcome like that from the statistics? If it had been a new Target, would there have been 50,000?

When a major employer with one of the worst reputations gets about 77 applicants for each job, what are we to think? It points clearly to one undocumented factor: latent demand. We live in a time when those who want jobs far exceed their supply. When a legitimate employer, criticized or not, offers 325 of them,

Status	Included in Census?	Labor Force Status	Listed as Wanting a Job?	Listed as Available to Work Now?
Unemployed	Yes	Included	Yes	Yes
Working Part Time for Economic Reasons	Yes	Included	N/A	N/A
Underemployed Due to Money, Skill, or Values	Yes	Included	N/A	N/A
Solidly Employed	Yes	Included	N/A	N/A
Discouraged	Yes	Marginally attached	Yes	Yes
Family Responsibilities	Yes	Marginally attached	Yes	No
In School or Training	Yes	Marginally attached	Yes	No
Ill Health or Disability	Yes	Marginally attached	Yes	No
Other	Yes	Marginally attached	Yes	No
Did Not Search For Work in Previous Year	Yes	Not included	Yes	Yes
Not Available to Work Now	Yes	Not included	Yes	No
Do Not Want a Job	Yes	Not included	No	No
Under Age 15	Yes	Not included	No	No
Non-Civilian and Institutionalized, 15+	Yes	Not included	No	No
American Expatriates	No	Not included	No	No

Figure 11: The 15 Different Employment Statuses and Where They Fit In

demand comes out of the woodwork. That is why any predictions of a labor shortage, for whatever reason, need to be offset dramatically.

A counterpart to latent demand is the tendency for companies to keep their top workers during bad times, even if they do not have enough for them to do. Though such employees will seemingly have no effect on unemployment, they represent excess capacity that must be consumed before others will be hired.[88]

Latent job demand is not limited to those who are officially unemployed, or even to those officially unemployed or discouraged. We cannot precisely assess just how many would be working in an era of plentiful jobs, but it is more than many realize. Such potential workers are more of the hidden casualties of Work's New Age. Is it a problem that they do not have jobs? Yes. If that would have been their first choice, it matters little whether they can work immediately or not—they have been damaged by the employment shortage. As *U.S. News & World Report* chief business correspondent Rick Newman put it, "We shouldn't declare a recovery until everybody who wants a job is at least looking for one."[89]

Fifty-Five Million More American Workers?

So how can we assign demand for jobs to the 15 categories? Let's start with two assumptions. First, I will name percentages based on a very strong labor market along a wide range of fields, one where almost anyone willing to work could find a job within a matter of weeks. The closest comparison in recent decades I know of was Houston in the early 1980s, when so many people moved there from manufacturing-declining Detroit that a newspaper's lead sentence said the hottest import there weighed only seven pounds and couldn't be driven: a Houston Sunday newspaper filled with job ads. Second, I will strive for conservatism.

Although those in the unemployed category are officially looking for work, some are there only briefly between jobs and some frankly prefer not to work, so I will estimate 90% would obtain employment. The three categories of people with jobs would be unchanged. Discouraged workers in a time of ample jobs would function much as those officially unemployed, so I have also assigned them 90%.

Those in the next set of statuses are smaller in number, but are harder to estimate with confidence. Those on the record as wanting to work but have stopped now due to family obligations would mostly continue them, but many would end up with jobs, so I will say 30% would take employment. While continuing school or seeking training is ostensibly a primary goal, many are there for lack of a paying alternative, so I estimate 50% of those would work. People with ill health or disabilities are mostly not able to take a job, but as we can understand from the rising number of disability applications, some would reach the labor force if they knew they could get employment, so I have included 10% as working. In the "other" grouping, I have estimated 30%.

In a job-seeker's market, those who did not search for work in the previous year but say they want jobs and are ready for them now would be similar to those officially unemployed. Since I think a significant number, though, would choose to continue not looking, I will assign 80% of them to finding work. Many of those "not available to work now," but still officially wanting jobs, would get them—I say about 30%.

How many people who are out of the labor force and claim not to want work would end up with it in a robust market? That is hard to tell. The great majority are fully retired, like or accept their lives as they are, and would not seek employment. However, people make plans, even long-term ones, based on what they consider to be realities. In the current market, many assume they could not get a reasonable job even if they wanted one, so we cannot dispose of the category entirely. With more than a quarter of the population, this is the largest single employment-status grouping, so small changes to the estimate would have a large effect on the number of potential employees. I have estimated that 5% of these people would get jobs if they thought they could, which, though possibly way too low, is unlikely to overstate.

We are left with the non-civilian and institutionalized category, of whom some in the armed services but few shut-ins might take jobs elsewhere, so I have assigned them 10%, and American expatriates, many of whom have left because of economic conditions at home, 20%. How about latent demand from other countries? During a strong employment market, pressure to limit immigration would lessen, so if the jobs were there maybe 100 million would move to America, of whom 30% would not be dependent family members and would work.

Figure 12 shows the 15 employment statuses of people in 2010, percent of the total population of American residents and expatriates, and number currently working in the United States,[90] along with these estimates of what percentage and number of people would accept a reasonably suitable job, with my guess of the number of possible immigrants at the bottom.

Fifty-five million more people working in America, with fewer than 15 million officially unemployed? It could happen, if getting a job were not much harder than buying a car. We have become used to expecting great difficulty selling our labor, which is getting ever harder as Work's New Age reveals itself.

The Job Market Affects More Than Just Unemployment

Although many people know better, the publicity of a statistic called "unemployment" can be deceptive, encouraging us to think that the only statistical effect of declining work opportunities is to increase that number. As we have seen, though, the number of jobs bears on other categories as well. When work becomes more available, many people out of the labor force join it, to become unemployed (looking for jobs), underemployed, or solidly employed, while some advance from unemployed to underemployed or solidly employed, and some move up from underemployed. When jobs become scarcer, the opposite happens: Solidly employed people become underemployed, unemployed, or leave the labor market entirely, whereas some underemployed lose their jobs or stop looking for them, and a number of unemployed give up the search as well. For example, in February 2011, unemployment dropped primarily due to people leaving the labor force.[91] Figures 13 and 14 show this pattern in diagrammatic form.

Status	Number in 2010	Percent of Total	Number Working in USA	Latent Demand Percent (Est.)	Latent Demand Number (Est.)
Unemployed	14,829,000	4.72%	0	90%	13,346,100
Working Part-Time for Economic Reasons	8,886,500	2.83%	8,886,500	–	0
Underemployed Due to Money, Skill, or Values	55,625,600	17.71%	55,625,600	–	0
Solidly Employed	74,551,900	23.73%	74,551,900	–	0
Discouraged	1,173,000	0.37%	0	90%	1,055,700
Family Responsibilities	286,000	0.09%	0	30%	85,800
In School or Training	350,000	0.11%	0	50%	175,000
Ill Health or Disability	50,000	0.02%	0	10%	5,000
Other	629,000	0.20%	0	30%	188,700
Did Not Search For Work in Previous Year	6,059,000	1.93%	0	80%	4,847,200
Not Available to Work Now	623,000	0.20%	0	30%	186,900
Do Not Want a Job	77,882,000	24.79%	0	5%	3,894,100
Under Age 15	62,142,928	19.78%	0	0%	0
Non-Civilian and Institutionalized, 15+	5,962,888	1.90%	0	10%	596,289
American Expatriates	5,000,000	1.59%	0	20%	1,000,000
Total	314,050,816	100.00%	139,064,000	–	25,380,789
Potential Immigrants	100,000,000	–	–	30%	30,000,000
Potential Total	414,050,816	–	–	–	55,380,789

Figure 12: The 15 Employment Categories Plus Potential Immigrants, with Total Numbers, Percentages, and Latent Demand for Jobs

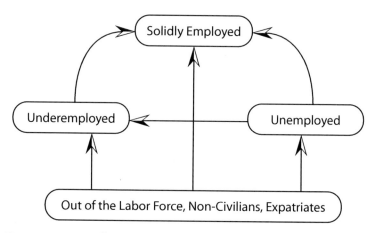

*Figure 13: Overall Model of Employment Status Movement—
More Jobs*

Upshot: The American Dream and Work's New Age

So how do we know the recent evidence of Work's New Age is not just from a recession and we'll be back to 5% unemployment before we know it? Federal Reserve Chairman Ben Bernanke predicted in January 2011 that the jobless rate would likely be about 8% two years later.[92] *U.S. News & World Report* editor Mortimer P. Zuckerman, who wrote in late 2010 that the country's nongovernmental employment "machine is clanging to a halt,"[93] claimed in early 2011, actually after a substantial drop in the monthly unemployment rate, that there was "no life in our jobs market," affirmed that "millions of men and women are willing and eager to work, but their skills, brainpower, and energies are wasted," and opined that though the Great Recession had ended, "the Great Job Recession continues apace."[94] Since 1980, the connection between large-company profitability and employment has been altered.[95] According to economist Robert J. Samuelson, "Companies are doing much better than workers; that's a defining characteristic of today's economy."[96] A Tom Toles cartoon in *The Washington Post* showed a formally dressed magician, "The Amazing Corporate America," after sawing a person

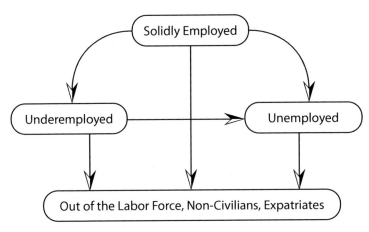

Figure 14: Overall Model of Employment Status Movement—
Fewer Jobs

marked "workforce," saying, "There is no 'rest of the trick.' I cut you in half and I got record profits!"[97] Another showed a sealed-off factory labeled, "The Economy" telling a mass of unemployed people outside, "Don't take this the wrong way, but we discovered it works better without you."[98]

Americans are discarding long-held views that the economy will be better for them than it was for their parents[99] and better for their children than it was for them[100]—indeed, the offspring of baby boomers will often be worse off.[101] As of August 2010, the United States economic condition was being described

> **WORK'S NEW AGE PRINCIPLE #1**
>
> **Profitable and growing companies do not consistently add workers anymore.**

by economists as "the new normal;"[102] two months later, Samuelson announced that "we have entered the Age of Austerity."[103] In Germany, a newspaper section-leading headline translated into "The End of the American Dream."[104] And former *New York Times* columnist Bob Herbert wrote in late 2010 that an economy facilitating jobs supporting reasonable living standards for all people who want them would constitute "a resurrection of the American dream."[105]

What is the American dream, anyway? If you ask ten people, you might get ten different answers, but they would be related. Some would say it is buying a house. Some would say it is getting married, having children, and living peacefully. Some would say it is being able to vote, to take part in the political system, and to freely criticize officeholders, candidates, and their actions or proposals. But one thing would come through. Few would mention wanting to be given things. Even the patent 19th-century exaggeration of American streets being paved with gold did not imply that anyone could pick it off the pavement. Those arriving at Ellis Island knew they would have to work.

America was the land of opportunity. Opportunity, not giveaways. Through most of its history, the country has offered a lot of it. Around 1900, Italians, Poles, Germans, and others willing to swing a hammer or push a shovel or bake a brick routinely found work—not easy, not always pleasant—and they found opportunity. European arrivals after World War II, if willing to first take positions not using their educations, could earn enough to support themselves. For most of the decades since, countries around the world have drained many brains, with the end of the largest pipe in central North America. Taxi drivers, janitors, and restaurant workers across the land offer not-so-mute testimony to the chances they have been given in the United States, with their prosperity, relatively low wages notwithstanding, vastly improved over what it was in Port-au-Prince, Dhaka, or Mexico City. Koreans in particular, if willing to work most of their waking hours, know they can build a life here, at convenience stores if nowhere else. At higher income levels, it is common to see Indian physicians, Russian rocket scientists, and Chinese information technology engineers, with incomes in particular and life amenities in general far better than most could get back home. And foreigners' overall success had not matched that achieved by natives, who after all grew up locally and at least in principle knew more about what in the country they could do best.

All of that is going away.

The time when old, new, and aspiring Americans can count on achieving what I maintain is the most common American dream, getting an opportunity to make a good life, is ending—permanently. We are now feeling the effect of Work's New Age: No longer will the number of American jobs approximate the number of those who can work them. If there was ever a reason for such a relationship, it is gone now, as the culture of work as we have known it is reaching a conclusion.[106] The economy may otherwise be good, bad, or indifferent, but as it now stands, from here on we will always have a group of those without jobs, which is likely to get ever larger, in our midst.[107] Why? We will see in Chapter 2.

Chapter 2:

It'll Get Worse

It's one thing for a nation to be downwardly mobile during a recession. It's quite another to be downwardly mobile during a recovery—but that looks to be precisely what's happening. —Harold Meyerson[108]

As before, recessions now normally end with unemployment levels still high. Indeed in 2004, before the 2008–2009 downturn and its worst one ever, a section heading in economist Jeremy Rifkin's *End of Work* was "The Permanent Jobless Recovery."[109] So why are all recoveries now jobless,[110] and why won't unemployment, and its varieties, improve greatly with better economic times?

Automation: Not Just a Future Fear Anymore

In the 1960s, "computer" became a household word, but not in the way those under 40 might think. Computers were large machines, often the size of rooms, used by government and large companies. Even in that decade, 20 years after IBM released ENIAC, they were not only working faster than humans but in a growing number of cases were cheaper too. A new fear began to spread: automation.

On March 22, 1964, a group called the Ad Hoc Committee on the Triple Revolution, including past and future Nobel Prize winners and *Scientific American* magazine's publisher, sent a letter to President Lyndon B. Johnson, expressing grave concern that computers, even as they were at the time, would soon cause large-scale joblessness.[111] The Commission on Automation, Technology, and Economic Progress, established by President Johnson, issued a report in which it disagreed that automation might remove vast numbers of jobs but acknowledged the possibility of significant societal and economic issues.[112] Norbert Wiener, an early commentator on automation, claimed that if its effects were not managed well, it could cause extreme unemployment.[113] Even a 1960s *MAD* magazine cartoon showed an angry boss telling an office worker he could be replaced by an IBM machine. It would only be a matter of time, many people then thought, until vast numbers of people, especially in wealthy and well-infrastructured America, would be automated out of their jobs.

That happened in numerous cases, but for a long time, automation did not materialize at anywhere near the level seen by its most pessimistic prognosticators. In 1969, 83 million Americans were employed, and in 1970, more than half of employed American adults had manual or clerical jobs.[114] Significant numbers of people with manufacturing positions lost them, but many found service work.[115] In the 1970s, jobs lost to improved technology were also largely or completely offset by employment growth elsewhere. Even in the 1980s, when personal computers became commonplace and office software such as spreadsheets and word processing programs became the norm, few positions actually disappeared, though in that decade American companies spent more than $1 trillion on computers, robots, and other mechanized equipment.[116] The 1990s brought controversy about how much work personal computers actually eliminated. The jobs remained. Later that decade, though, automation worries became more justified. Secretaries shrank in number and in many workplaces almost disappeared. Many clerical functions such as making copies, distributing documents, and the keying that replaced typing ceased to be done by a central support person and were completed by the formerly-requesting managers themselves. Telephone messages moved from secretaries' responsibilities to desktop answering machines to phone-connecting software and voicemail. Entire sets of workers such as telephone operators, despite their products and services being used more, saw their numbers vastly reduced or eliminated completely. In some situations, the efficiency was offset by increases; for example, while between 1980 and 2000 automation allowed an average mutual fund accountant to cover four of them instead of one or two, the number of such funds increased tenfold.[117] American business was generally good in the 1990s, which masked much of technology's effect on employment.

Although outsourcing, or the departure of jobs to other companies or countries, was much more publicized in the mid-1990s than automation, in 1994 economists Paul Krugman and Robert Lawrence said that automation was the greater threat.[118] The next year, Jeremy Rifkin wrote about "intelligent machines replacing human beings in countless tasks" and of millions of jobs, no longer cost-effective when compared with machines, disappearing.[119] He documented automation and its resulting reduction of human work in a wide range of industries—appliances, automobile manufacturing, banking, chemical refining, electronics, food service, insurance, mining, office work, professional fields, retail sales, rubber, steel, and textiles[120]—and noted that in one four-year period, 1989 to 1993, 1.8 million manufacturing workers had lost their jobs.[121] Over all, in 2000, 135 million Americans were working, almost 25% at manual positions and about 14% apiece at service, clerical, and managerial spots,[122] but by the early 21st century, the old fear of automation had become even more justified. Duties performed by computers as of 2004 included filing, bookkeeping, assessment of mortgage suitability, order-taking, and robotic work in the automobile industry and elsewhere.[123] Around that time, mechanization was replacing about 7 million positions each year.[124]

Since 2001, many fields have shed jobs to automation much more sophisticated than before. Pharmacists are moving from filling prescriptions themselves to supervising the work of others, that verification made easier through number-coded medicines.[125] Much work of property assessors is now done by programs which use algorithmic data such as rooms, neighborhood statistics, square feet, and so on.[126] Accountants now similarly hand over their least judgment-requiring tasks.[127] Software to access multiple databases has replaced some business analysts, and diagnostic packages have cut the number of doctors.[128] Up to 50% of employed commercial artists and advertising designers have been replaced, while expert computer systems have been able to generate materials they previously prepared.[129] Automated supermarket checkout lines have appeared, endangering the work of what in 2006 were almost 3.5 million American cashiers.[130] In January 2011, a company evaluated 1.5 million legal papers for under $100,000, using advanced document analyzing software that could potentially replace 500 lawyers with one.[131] In what may seem like almost a parody of automation, elementary school teaching robots, with human faces on their head-like monitors and remote-controlled by those in cheaper-labor countries, have made their debut in some Korean public schools.[132] At the same time, from 2000 to 2010, automation was partially or wholly responsible for the loss of 5.6 million jobs in manufacturing alone,[133]

> ## WORK'S NEW AGE PRINCIPLE #2
>
> **Major future inventions will have nowhere near the employment-boosting effect as cars, electricity, or television did in the past, as their work processes will be far too automated.**

and in 2004 Jeremy Rifkin estimated that 90 million jobs, or more than 70% of the number of people in the workforce, were at risk to be mechanized away.[134] In 2011 Mortimer P. Zuckerman saw the risks of automation to be so great that it could destabilize the entire country.[135] Yet software development company founder Martin Ford, author of *The Lights in the Tunnel,* maintained in 2009 that economists still considered technology-caused high unemployment to be "unthinkable."[136]

The future promises to hold even more of the same. Tasks now ripe for automation include auditing, more teaching, and more health care providing.[137] For one, radiologists, whose work is mostly pattern recognition in a controlled environment,[138] may become far fewer. In general, higher-paid positions where accumulated knowledge can be defined algorithmically may be hit hardest by automation.[139] More high-powered technical positions will be invented and filled, but their numbers will be dwarfed by those they and their machines replaced.[140] Search engine optimizing, named by journalist, columnist, and author Thomas Friedman as an example of something in which America could specialize,[141] would not employ one percent of the number of autoworkers two generations ago, and the labor force today is much larger. Any commonly adopted products, on a par with the popularity of radio or TV, would create jobs, but would be too automated in their production to employ great masses.[142] For example, as of 2010, the companies of eBay, Facebook, and Twitter, some of the most popular innovations of the past two decades, employed 17,000, 2,000, and 300 people, respectively.[143] Ultimately, as Martin Ford, who called such positions "software jobs," put it, "At some point in the future—it might be many years or decades from now—machines will be able to do the jobs of a large percentage of the 'average' people in our population, and these people will *not* be able to find new jobs."[144]

Work responsibilities in the process of automation often go through a series of phases. At first, the job has no real technical component—wages are low, skills needed to perform it are modest or easily learned, and the number of people doing it, per unit of business volume, reaches its highest point. Second, machines to help the job, which the average worker can run, are developed and replace manual means. Farmers get tractors instead of plows, miners use augers instead of picks and shovels, and invoice clerks change from writing by hand to using typewriters. As a result, productivity increases—the number of employees required, at a given production level, drops—and wages go up while prices may come down. At this point, demand for the product or service may increase so much that even more workers will be needed to cover it, so there will be little perception that improved efficiency is costing jobs. As an example, AT&T had a similar number of telephone operators in 1990 as in 1940, but the calling volume was then so much greater that, according to one senior manager, had the level of automation stayed the same, all the women in the United States from ages 18 to 65 would have been needed to handle the calls.

Third, a new generation of machines is implemented for a further fundamental gain in productivity, but they are too sophisticated for the average holder of the position to operate effectively. Typists get word processors, warehouse workers get computer inventory systems, and auto mechanics get various automated tools. Unless product or service demand continues to increase, jobs are lost, and since the employees must now have more knowledge and skill, wages rise again. In many cases, this is the point when observers realize that fewer people are working at this occupation, and though automation has been happening for some time, they comment on how it is affecting employment. Life is good for those still in the field, but all know there are fewer of them.

The fourth phase happens when the machines are able to take over the work entirely and the jobs disappear. Many industries were in this phase as of 2004, when productivity gains were consistently accompanied by job losses.[145] A graphic example of the fourth phase was provided by MIT and Harvard economists Frank Levy and Richard J. Murnane of traders on the London International Financial Futures and Options Exchange, earning as much as $450,000 annually in the mid-1990s and completely replaced by a computer network in 1999.[146] A few of the many other jobs essentially mechanized away over the years were copy clerks, icemen, payroll clerks, bowling pin boys, calculators and equation-solvers, lamplighters, and wheelwrights.

There are still some key limits to automation. Computers excel at linear tasks, involving numeric calculations and yes-no logical operators or those involving following unambiguous rules.[147] Since soon after ENIAC, they have had this type of processing power exceeding that in any human brain. Their algorithm skills are currently so potent that some are unbeatable at checkers,[148] and they can beat human chess champions through quickly evaluating literally millions of board positions and consequences of possible moves.[149] Yet many chores easy even for small children still elude effective completion by robots or computers.[150] When robots have been installing automotive components for decades we may think they can identify and retrieve an ordinary book from a household table in a typical home, which most five-year-olds can easily do, but they cannot. A robot can only install, say, a car window when the auto frame is in a precise location, of an exact type, and the path to it is unimpeded. By contrast, even a six-year-old understands that what constitutes a "book" takes in a variety of appearances and states. A book can be the size of a credit card, or a few square feet in surface area. It can be paperback or hardcover and of any color. It can be almost cardboard-thin or several inches thick. It can be face up, face down, spine up, open or closed. All of that of course only covers the book and not the "table," a concept which includes its own variability of location, size, height, and range of places on which the book can rest. The trip back and forth from the table may require detours away from things near the ground (a rideable toy car), deviations at or above eye level (other furniture), and things that while relatively small should be detoured around (a sleeping dog). Some objects, while significant in size, would require no alternate routing, since they can be safely stepped over (a large wooden toy block), while some detours may be needed away from spaces not even then occupied (a perception that if one moved forward she would collide with someone moving into the area from another direction). The floor or carpet surface could be wet, dry, or impeded by rugs that would call for slower movement. Furthermore, the child could determine for some reason, such as a physical confrontation between others in the room, that the task could not then be safely completed and might instead correctly choose to report that instead of endangering herself or others. As long as identifying what constitutes a book, a table, an impediment requiring an alternative route, differing floor conditions, and a justifiable need to not complete a task remain to our understanding non-algorithmic, technology will not be able to replace humans in finishing it, and jobs requiring such skills, however modest, will not all be mechanized away. Housekeepers will be much more resistant to automation than radiologists.[151]

One more set of jobs has been necessary to connect human work with computers. I worked as a data-entry clerk in the late 1980s. My entire responsibility was connecting other people's writing, in this case on forms for paying bills to AT&T's suppliers, to electronic systems. Now that task is done at the source, with those generating and authorizing bills entering them directly, without paper. Much other work, such as that performed by a bank loan agency, involves collecting information from humans and arranging its automated input.[152] In numerous cases, such as with paying AT&T's bills, elimination of these connective positions awaits only capability for data to be collected at the source in a mechanized fashion.

So what might be the future of automation limitations? Some may depend on how, if at all, we can break down more and more tasks into algorithms. Once we understand how to quantify patterns, they can be mechanized. Such initial effort may be labor intensive, as information must be broken down into tiny pieces which, when combined, must add up correctly to what a good human worker would perceive. Robots, now available for relatively controlled, homogeneous tasks and environments, such as cutting grass in a lawn of programmable size or cleaning industrial floors,[153] will become able to do more and more chores in more and more settings. The environments themselves may be made more suitable for automata, as above by standardizing items and their positions and removing obstacles, allowing, for example, mechanized restocking of supermarket shelves.[154] Also it is probable that robots and their directing computers will be better suited to overcoming obstacles than they are now. None of that considers the possibility of a true breakthrough in computing, perhaps along the lines of "fuzzy logic," allowing machines to expand beyond their unambiguous-task limitation.

What are the results when automation helps but cannot completely replace people? One has been not to eliminate jobs but to reduce their numbers, moving human practitioners into supervisory or cross-checking roles. The pharmacists above are one example. Although far fewer are needed, there still must be some, since prescriptions cannot be dispensed without their confirmation of correctness. In this case the technology does not replace all pharmacists; it only allows those remaining to do several times as much work apiece as before.

A second form is computer output increasing a worker's productivity but without other humans being involved. Auto mechanics have some of the most resistant jobs to overall automation, as the work is physical and quite variable,[155] yet they can do more work in less time when computers assess certain problems. The second and third automation phases above usually have this result. In these cases, the workers may become more valued and become better paid, and if automation thus leads to lower prices and increased sales, it may actually cause companies to hire more.[156]

A third result is one not necessarily related to decreased employment, because it involves not making work faster or more efficient but improving its quality. One example is the use of comprehensive information-providing software in cardiology, in which the knowledge does not allow for fewer cardiologists but provides them a basis for better decisions.[157]

Some jobs will remain untouched by automation— but very few. Even taxi drivers are made more efficient by GPS devices. Yet Kurt Vonnegut Jr.'s *Player Piano*, a 1952 novel about a future with few workers needed, described manicure and barbering machines programmed by recording the exact movements of skilled human practitioners.[158]

So how are people adapting to increasing automation? For one, in many cases, we are already seeing higher employee competition for jobs that seem to have low chances of being mechanized away.[159] The joke of a plumber, when questioned about his asking $125 for a short visit by being told the householder, a lawyer, didn't charge that much, saying, "I know; that's why I stopped practicing law," may become too realistic to elicit many laughs.

Any discussion of automation would be incomplete if it did not mention what might be called the nuclear bomb of mechanization, the Singularity. According to inventor and futurist Ray Kurzweil, who has written extensively on this potential phenomenon, "Within several decades information-based technologies will encompass all human knowledge and proficiency, ultimately including the pattern-recognition powers, problem-solving skills, and emotional and moral intelligence of the human brain itself."[160] If the Singularity occurs, which as of 2005 Kurzweil estimated will happen by 2045, there will be no meaningful line between humans and machines.[161] I liken it to a nuclear blast, since it would obliterate so much of our lifestyles that if it does happen, it might not matter whether there are any jobs or not. If people survive indefinitely, although in a quasi-machine state, relatively minor considerations such as whether they could also work would become quite peripheral quite suddenly. In any event, we should not use its possibility as a device to abdicate our awareness of automation as the largest single cause of Work's New Age.

Scalability: When a Million Takes Barely More Labor Than a Thousand

In the pre-industrial age, the world contained far fewer people. The planet's population, now seven times this number, did not reach even one billion until 1850, decades after Watt's steam engine had transformed the Western world. Before that event, production of few goods was scalable, meaning that every barrel, plow, or kitchen knife was made by hand. Every bushel of wheat came from a farm with equipment primitive by modern standards. If you wanted 100 cooking kettles, they would require close to 100 times as much time and labor as one.

Of an item that took about an hour to produce in a pre-industrial setting, say a set of shoes for one specific horse, how much time would be needed to make 10, 100, or 1,000? The blacksmith would need some setup time before he could start working, maybe 15 minutes. After that, the first set might take an hour. By the time the blacksmith made 10 sets, he would have gained information on how to make them more quickly and would need no more setup time, so each one would take, say, 10% less time or 54 minutes apiece. By 100, he would have found even more ways to save time, so each set might be down to 85% of the hour or 51 minutes. At 1,000, the smith would be the world's foremost expert at making shoes for that particular animal, so could be expected to take maybe 48 minutes. Figure 15 shows this progression graphically.

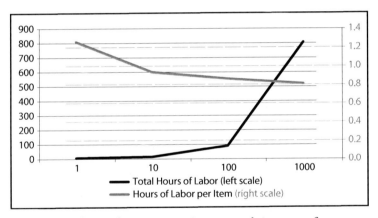

Figure 15: Relationship Between Output and Amount of Labor Required, by Number of Items Produced —Pre-Industrial

The advent and proliferation of machines changed the equation. More things could be made in less time apiece, but it took significant time and labor to set up a factory and to start and stop a production run. Problem identification and resolution would make manufacturing more efficient as time went on, but only after a substantial quantity of items were made. To produce 100 Model T Ford automobiles might take 6,000 person-hours, but 1,000 might take only 40,000, and 10,000 might be completed with 300,000 hours of labor. The Industrial Revolution, therefore, changed the relationship of things made to hours needed from almost linear to exponential.

So let's use a classic 20th-century factory to make some can openers. We'll need a lot more setup time to design the product, get the workers to understand it, implement the specifications, prepare the assembly line, and so on—we'll call it 200 hours. After that, though, the can openers will take only 15 minutes of labor apiece. Unlike the horseshoes, they won't have much for improvements until a larger number have been made, say 100, but by the time we've made 1,000 the process should be a little bit better, so each one might take only 24/100ths of an hour. The chart then looks like this:

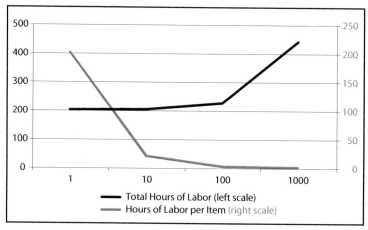

Figure 16: Relationship Between Output and Amount of Labor Required, by Number of Items Produced—Industrial

The post-industrial age brought in products with even higher startup times and even lower marginal labor needs. Microsoft's Word software has taken thousands upon thousands of hours to develop. If the company had a market for only one Word user, for Microsoft to make money he or she would have to pay millions of dollars. But it's not like that, with tens of millions of copies of Word sold annually in America alone. Each additional one requires at most a CD, paper, case, and packing, all mass-produced and hardly related to the actual product cost. With so much of the expense being up front, incremental sales have colossal gross margins, maybe $99 of each $100.

So it's the early 21st century and we are now making software. With programming, debugging, testing, optimizing, user acceptance and more, none of which we want to do after production starts, the setup time is tremendous; it might be 10,000 hours before the first sale-ready copy is made. After that, though, the cost will be tiny, say 0.01 hour of labor per unit. So our chart comes out as this:

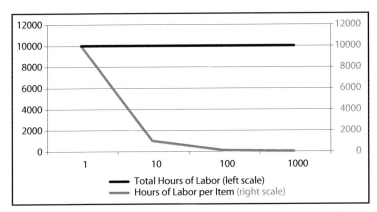

Figure 17: Relationship Between Output and Amount of Labor Required, by Number of Items Produced
—Post-Industrial

There are many other products with very high origination costs and low marginal costs, some of them relatively new in their current forms and all benefiting from post-industrial technology. Two examples are casino gambling, where the cost of building is gigantic but more people coming in cost Harrah's or MGM

Mirage almost nothing, and long-distance telephone service over a network such as AT&T's, which can accommodate vastly more calls than are ever made at almost no extra expense after having cost well into the billions.

With the change from industrial to post-industrial production, the relationship between labor and value created has moved from exponential to logarithmic. Logarithms are the value of exponents. For example, 10 to the 2nd power, or 100, has a base 10 logarithm of 2, whereas 10 to the 4th power, or 10,000, has logarithm 4. If Microsoft uses 40,000 hours of labor to produce 10,000 copies of Word, it may well need only 60,000 for one million, or 90,000 for one billion. Imagine that with horseshoes!

Businesses vary greatly in how much in sales they have per employee, a key indicator of scalability. As of 2008, McDonalds, offering manufactured products distributed with sizable labor per unit value, had revenue of about $59,000 per employee. Wal-Mart, also selling manufactured goods but with lower worker involvement per unit, was much higher, at $180,000. Intel, producing chips with low size and weight but high value, sold about $456,000 per employee, and Microsoft, with perhaps the classic set of scalable modern products, had $664,000.[162] Google, whose goods and services take up no physical space other than the computing equipment they need and which can be produced in quantity for close to no marginal cost at all,[163] had more than a million dollars in average sales per worker.[164]

> **WORK'S NEW AGE PRINCIPLE #3**
>
> Automation and scalability each damage the connection between work and consumption; their combination destroys it.

Combining scalability with automation gives us two dimensions. On one axis, we have the potential for automation, which can be quite low in some cases and much higher in others. On the other axis, there are products with low scalability on one end and those much more scalable on the

	Low Automatability	High Automatability
High Scalability	Initial Electronic Production (creating online advertising, electronic greeting cards, software, or capability for telephone calls)	Electronic Distribution (selling items on the left once they have been created)
Low Scalability	Haircuts Massages Restaurant Meals City Driving Building Construction Most Personal Services	Farming Mining Most Manufacturing Most Computer-to-Computer Interface Services

Figure 18: Goods and Services by Automatability and Scalability

other. In Figure 18 we see how a matrix of products on these two dimensions might look in 2012.

One feature of automation and scalability is that when combined, they eventually obliterate the connection between work and consumption. When another million people buy the latest Microsoft Office, the number of workers needed to handle this extra business relative to Microsoft's revenues is tiny. When the labor component of prices becomes smaller and smaller, increased sales cause fewer and fewer people to be hired.[165] The Luddite Fallacy, named after a British 1811 anti-technology movement, holds that mechanistic progress will never cause widespread unemployment.[166] Two hundred years later, the Luddite Fallacy is still, in the main, correct—as of early 2011, nominal unemployment rates were about 9%, not 75%. But we cannot make the thoughtless assumption that because it hasn't happened yet it never will; the huge consumer spending of the mid-2000s may have further delayed, among other factors, obvious effects of automation.[167] As Martin Ford put it, "Technology isn't going to stand still while we wait for the job market to recover."[168] What can we do if we see the likes of 75% unemployment? I will discuss that matter in chapters to come. In the meantime, while many jobs will remain, automation and scalability, even if no other factors could be considered, are reasons enough to explain Work's New Age.

Health Insurance: An Ever-More-Expensive Albatross

A long time ago, when someone went to the doctor or hospital, they paid in full. Sometimes they provided the money later, sometimes if the bill was large they paid it over time, and sometimes if they didn't have much they might have given whatever they had: food, farm animals, or other goods or services. Sometimes, as now, they didn't pay at all. Yet there was no concept of someone else covering it, any more than for today's trips to the grocery store or laundromat.

Employee sickness funds, to which employees paid insurance premiums in order to be compensated for workdays missed, had been in America at least as far back as 1901.[169] What may have been the first employer-based American health insurance plan was the sickness fund offered to employees of Huyck and Sons, a Rensselaer, New York, company making papermakers' felts, in 1911.[170] The idea spread quickly, and as of 1916, 8 million American men would be paid insurance money for days they were sick.[171]

Still, as late as the 1930s, most health services were paid directly by patients.[172] The first wider-range American employee health plan started in 1929, when some Dallas teachers worked with local Baylor University Hospital, getting a system which provided up to three weeks' hospitalization annually for a monthly premium of 50 cents. In 1937, after other hospitals began offering similar plans, Blue Cross started operations, and in 1939 Blue Shield, which covered other doctor's bills, did the same.[173] In 1940, Blue Cross claimed more than 6 million enrollees in 39 different hospital-controlled programs.[174] The Internal Revenue Service helped health insurance spread further by ruling that employers could deduct its cost as a business expense as with cash compensation, but employees needed to pay no taxes on it either. Through World War II, the government decreed ceilings on wages and prices but exempted the cost of employee benefits up to 5% of pay, a limit then well above the cost of health insurance.[175] In the absence of raises, more and more employers offered health plans, which covered 7 million people at war's beginning and 26 million by its end,[176] at which time they had completely replaced employee sickness funds.[177] The 20% of the population the 26 million represented leapt to 60% by 1954.[178]

In 1960, medical care made up 5.1% of American gross domestic product, or GDP.[179] In 1965, although Medicare was not yet enacted, 70% of Americans had some form of hospitalization insurance.[180] When Medicare passed that year, one condition that lawmakers deemed necessary for its approval was satisfying doctors and hospitals by allowing them, as was the case with most private plans, to collect charges that were "usual and customary" in their geographic areas.[181] Mean physician income soon reached an all-time peak of $32,170,[182] and for-profit hospitals went into business that decade also.[183] Total medical expenditures went way up, increasing from $27 billion in 1960 to $73 billion in 1970,[184] when they reached 7.4% of GDP.[185] By that year, 80% of Americans were covered for hospital bills and surgery, and just over half had insurance paying at least some share of office visits.[186]

The 1970s saw the first health management organizations, or HMOs.[187] By 1980, total health care spending had reached $257 billion[188] or 9.2% of GDP,[189] and achieved 10% in 1982.[190] During the decade, HMOs became more proprietary than hospitals—while 12% of HMOs were for profit in 1981, 50% were in 1986.[191] The proportion of employers' health care expenses to payroll increased from 5.0% in 1976 to 9.7% in 1988,[192] with its cost soaring 18.6% in 1988 and another 20.4% in 1989.[193] By 1990, health care expenses were 12.2% of GDP.[194]

By the late 1990s, health care costs were rising much faster than inflation.[195] Those registered in HMOs, 6 million in 1976, increased every year until reaching 81.1 million in 1999, then dropped to 71.8 million in 2003.[196] All forms of managed care (systems in which insurers participate actively in decisions by approving or declining procedures, choosing medications, controlling the length of hospital stays, and so on), including preferred provider organizations (PPOs) as well as HMOs, grew from 5% of covered employees in 1980[197] to 95% in 1990.[198] In 1998, only 18% of health expenses were paid directly by patients.[199] In the same year, American medical spending was 13.6% of GDP,[200] and in 1999 its total reached $1.2 trillion.[201]

By 2000, 64% of Americans had health care coverage through work.[202] Between 2000 and 2005, employer family coverage premiums rose an average of 73%, while wages increased only 15%,[203] and health care spending per privately-insured person increased an average of 8.6% per year, more than twice the rise in per-capita GDP.[204] Between the same years, the mean cost to employers per policy increased to $3,991, up 32.5% even after inflation,[205] and health care coverage's share of overall payroll cost increased from 8% to 11%.[206] In 2005, health spending was 16% of GDP and just short of $2 trillion, which it reached the next year.[207] In 2010 it represented 17% of GDP.[208]

Health care expenses for employers are continuing to rise. After premiums grew an average of 6.0% in 2009 and 6.9% in 2010, they were expected to climb 8.8% more in 2011. An owner of a 100-person company reported that between 2009 and 2010 his costs increased nearly 25%, even by using the cheapest of many alternatives, as his previous provider more than doubled its rates.[209] In addition, workers also paid an average of $1,965 in 2009 and $2,209 in 2010 for premiums alone,[210] and the mean employee out-of-pocket cost of copays, coinsurance, and deductibles was expected to increase from $1,935 in 2010 to $2,177 in 2011. Altogether, employers' average per-worker health care share will have progressed from $4,083 in 2001 to $9,821 in 2011, with the employees' piece, jumping from $1,229 to $4,386,[211] expected to cause workers more and more problems.[212] These high and fast-increasing health care expenses discourage employers from hiring[213] and dismay employees as well. As for the future, one August 2010 set of projections showed average total inflation-adjusted compensation increasing significantly over the next three decades, but all of the gain to be accounted for by rising health insurance costs.[214]

The health care changes made law in 2010 will alter some aspects of employer-provided insurance. Starting in 2014 businesses with one to 100 workers, and larger ones in 2017, will be able to combine with others in "exchanges," statewide insurance markets which legislators hope will allow them to pay lower rates through insurance-provider competition and economies of scale.[215] However, employers will incur fines if any of their workers receive government subsidies toward their insurance purchased through an exchange, which could happen if the employer's health plan pays less than 60% of covered expenses or if the employee's insurance share exceeds 9.5% of their wages.[216] Companies must also provide vouchers to assist many workers whose insurance premiums are at least 8% of their income, or incur other financial penalties.[217] Employee health plans also must cover workers' dependent children up to age 26, and firms will lose tax deductions on retirees' prescription drug outlays, which will have an impact so large that some employers have already taken substantial tax write-offs.[218] Companies will be enjoined to provide health care within 90 days for all new hires, and those with more than 200 full-time workers must automatically enroll new employees as well.[219] However, existing health care plans will not need to comply with many of the law's modifications, though what exactly constitutes a new plan has not yet been established.[220]

Over the past few decades, the ever-rising cost of health care has greatly weighed down the cost of employment and prevented untold numbers of jobs from being offered and filled. Will the new health care laws, if they are not repealed or heavily modified, stop medical costs from increasing as dramatically? Or is American health care on a spiral, perhaps powered by allowing ever-increasing "reasonable and customary" rates, which can only be ended through stronger action? We will consider the last possibility in Chapter 7.

Efficiencies in Bad Times and Good

In Copenhagen several years ago I stopped at a gas station. As with the American variety, it had several pumps of different grades, and diesel as well as unleaded. As in the United States, the station took credit cards. In fact, it accepted nothing else. Why? There were no people working there! Why not? Labor costs are higher in Denmark than in America, and this way they were minimized. Barring remodeling or other major changes, one person could easily manage ten or more such stations. So what is to stop such from becoming common in the United States? American ones are now almost convenience stores first and make more money on a cup of coffee than a tank of unleaded. But even those have no more employees, typically two or three at a time for a dozen-pump installation, than did stations which offered only gas, oil, and other small car-related services a few decades ago.

Other than eliminating employees almost entirely, one business practice that requires fewer workers, called "lean production,"[221] is designed to get advantages of mass manufacturing with fewer regular employees.[222] The result of lean production is often a group of core, permanent workers, with contract and temporary labor added as needed.[223] The core employees must know more about a variety of tasks and be prepared for changing roles.[224] A related technique, practiced by Microsoft, among others, is the same except to keep the non-company-employed workers longer, which helps the company save money on benefits and possibly salaries.

It is common for organizations, when forced to reduce staff, to find that work can be completed successfully by fewer people. As times improve, the lost jobs may not come back. The same can hold for implementing software and robots in response to financial problems, a consideration projected by some to be large in the 2008–2009 recession's recovery.[225] Indeed, corporate sales at the end of 2010 had returned to the same point as in mid-2009, but 5% of company jobs had disappeared.[226] If you think back to your experiences of being short on time, money, or other resources and making changes in what you did and how you did things, you probably remember improvements that were so good you kept them even when the time or money returned. Businesses do that too.

A High Supply of Workers and Lower Demand for Them Means What?

Between 1947 and 1973, in the Winning by Default Years when, as before, America had little competition in many large industries, median family income in constant dollars doubled.[227] From 1973 to 1995 it stayed the same.[228] In 2003, average actual-dollar pay for office and factory non-supervisors increased three cents per hour, the lowest amount since the early 1960s.[229] As of January 2011, 40% of jobs lost in the 2008–09 recession were in higher-paying industries. After it ended, though, only 14% of those created after it ended were, and businesses where work paid below an average of $15 per hour accounted for 23% of jobs lost during the recession but 49% of new ones afterward.[230] Thirty-three percent of new jobs created from January 2010 through January 2011 were with temporary help firms.[231]

> **WORK'S NEW AGE PRINCIPLE #4**
>
> Efficiencies discovered during bad times carry on to good times.

Since the 1970s, employee benefits have become less common. Of private company workers 18 to 64 years old and putting in at least 20 hours per week and half the weeks in a year, 69.0% were covered by health insurance in 1979, which dropped in 1989, 2000, and 2006 to 61.5%, 58.9%, and 55.0%, respectively.[232] For the same set of workers and years, 50.6%, 43.7%, 48.3%, and 42.8% were covered by either pensions or 401(k)s.[233] Smaller-company employees often lost health coverage—from 2000 to 2005, the share of employers with fewer than 200 workers offering health insurance dropped from 68% to 59%,[234] and between 2005 and 2008 the number of businesses with 10 or fewer employees providing it plunged from 48.2% to 18.6%.[235] In the late 2000s, companies began reacting to worsening business conditions and possibly also to the high unemployment rate. From October 2008 to September 2009, American businesses collectively ended 50 pension plans, and at the end of that time 260,000 fewer workers had them. In 2009, the number of 401(k) plans nationwide actually increased by 74, but 700,000 fewer employees were enrolled.[236] Of large companies surveyed in 2010, in the previous two years 18% had reduced or totally removed their employee retirement plan contributions.[237]

So how much more productive has American business become in relation to jobs? From 1980 to 2000, workplace productivity steadily rose, while inflation-adjusted earnings for 80% of workers dropped.[238] Between June and September 2003, economic growth reached a 19-year high, but the total number of jobs decreased by 146,000.[239] Calculations for Okun's Law, an algorithm to determine unemployment using production levels, show that given productivity at the end of 2009, the unemployment rate should have been about 8.3% instead of the 10% it was.[240] From 2009 to 2010, when unemployment went over 10%, productivity increased much faster than labor expenses, up 5.2%, with pay up only 0.3%,[241] and in 2010 reached an eight-year high,[242] while cash compensation did not increase.[243] From September 1999 to May 2010, the economy grew by 20%, while the number of jobs stayed the same.[244] Ultimately, companies have

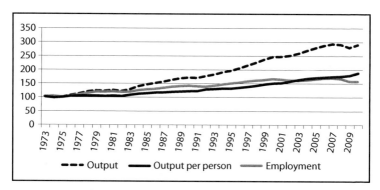

Figure 19: Productivity Indexes—Output, Output per Person, and Employment (1973=100). 1947–1972 averages: Output 59.6, Output per Person 71.3, Employment 82.4

discovered that they not only need fewer workers but can hire and retain them for less.[245]

Figure 19 shows trends in output, output per person, and employment, normalized to values of 100 for 1973.[246] Output as used above is gauged from weighted indexes provided by various industries, usually incorporating inflation-adjusted sales figures.[247] Note that output has gone well past both of the other two variables, showing that making things in general requires fewer and fewer workers, and that while employment in 2010 approximated those working in 1996, output per person has risen greatly since then.

As lower wages are a natural response to high unemployment,[248] more and more new jobs offer reduced pay and benefits. Sometimes the results disappoint employers when they do not get the workers they need, such as in 2010, when a company in Illinois offered capable machinists $13.00 per hour, well below common rates. Corporations have offered work in other countries for less than it pays in the United States and have also had few takers, as with a Dubai airline offering $30,000 per year in 2010 for American nationals to work in the United Arab Emirates.[249] In some cases, employers are negotiating with unions to reduce wages. In October 2010, General Motors and the United Auto Workers (UAW) worked out a two-tiered pay plan for employees at a Michigan plant in which all would keep their positions, but the bottom 40% in seniority would be paid $14.00 per hour, half of that for those with more seniority, for an overall 20% pay cut. UAW members accepted the plan, probably since they knew that in any event the old wage for the newer workers was gone, and their choice was either to work for lower pay or lose their jobs.[250]

What is the current status of employee benefit packages? As of March 2010, 50% of private-industry workers participated in either pensions or 401(k) equivalents, and 51% had some health care coverage, of which employers paid an average of 80% of the total premium costs for single-person coverage and 70% of those for families. Fifty-six percent were provided life insurance. The shares of private-company workers with paid sick leave, paid vacations, and paid personal leave were 62%, 77%, and 37%, respectively.[251]

As we know, when supply for something is higher than demand, its prices usually drop. So why haven't there been even more wage reductions? The difference is that individual workers are not commodities ignorant to changes in their valuation; morale, damaged even among surviving workers when others are cut,[252] is a value, and losing a top performer because of a periodic downward compensation adjustment would not be fully corrected by hiring a replacement.[253] So to minimize morale worsening, many employers have preferred to lay off less-needed workers and maintain existing pay and benefits for the others.[254] Therefore, we must take seriously the reductions in compensation we have seen and realize that with time there will be many more.

As with other efficiencies, pay and benefit cuts are often not restored even when business improves. In particular, in the late 2000s many companies that reduced 401(k) matching funds when business was bad failed to reinstate them when profitability improved.[255] So how are workers reacting? Journalist and author Daniel Gross said in 2010 that they were "sick and tired of tough conditions and crummy salaries."[256] That year, a staggering 48% expected to seek new employment when the economy improved. But workers may not be able to leave or negotiate more freely until unemployment rates drop below 7%.[257] If that does not happen, they will have decisions to make. Over all, on pay and benefits, the free market is now speaking.

No, All Those Baby Boomers Will <u>Not</u> Be Retiring

American baby boomers are usually considered those born between 1946 and 1964. The first turned 65 at the beginning of 2011, and many commentators have claimed that their retirement in large numbers will free up enough jobs to end any employment problems, or to even create a labor shortage.[258] The data says otherwise.

Why do people choose to retire? The two most common reasons have historically been wellness-related and financial: The better health and less money someone has, the less likely they are to retire, with healthiness being by far the most significant predictor.[259]

Because of improved nutrition, ways of daily life, and exercise,[260] those turning 65 may have the vitality of previous 50-year-olds.[261] Financially, though, the baby boom generation is in serious trouble. Even before the 2008–2009 recession, they as a group had saved less than previous cohorts, and many rated to find retiring at 65 unattractive or even impossible.[262] The national average savings rate, 7.0% in 1990, fell to 6.0% in 1995, 2.3% in 2000, and 1.2% in 2004,[263] showing that during baby boomers' peak earning years, Americans were keeping less and less. A 2004 study showed the mean net worth for people aged 35 to 44 (those born from about 1960 to 1969) and 45 to 54 (those born 1950 to 1959) to have been $77,600 and $132,000, respectively,[264] significant money but dependent on further contributions beyond Social Security to fund a comfortable retirement. In 2006, more than 90% of my post-65 survey respondents reported they would be more likely to take on career jobs, not just jobs, if they had less money.[265] Many are in that situation now.

Since then, studies have shown that baby boomers felt more financially damaged by the 2008–2009 recession than any other age group. Many were counting on home equity in particular to facilitate their retirements—with average 2008-2010 housing prices dropping more than 30%,[266] a large number lost all they had. Older employees' workforce participation and unemployment both reached all-time highs in 2010,[267] when in November mean unemployment time for those 55 and older was 45 weeks, 12 higher than for those younger.[268] Late that year, roughly 60% of 50- to 61-year-old study respondents reported they had decided to retire later than they previously thought, while 35% of those over 61 had already put it off.[269] Over all, Rick Newman's early 2010 assessment that most

Americans might want to work for 10 to 15 years later than previous generations[270] seems well justified.

Baby boomers have long had different views on aging from those before. In a 2002 survey, 60% of them aged 48 and older and 65% of those younger said they expected to work part time after retirement.[271] An AARP study from 2003, half a decade before the housing and stock market price drop, showed only 20% considered retirement time unproductive.[272] As well, longevity at age 65 has increased from 14.4 years in 1960 to 17.6 years in 2000,[273] and is expected to reach 18.5 in 2020.[274] Financial problems aside, longer life expectancy alone may be reason enough for baby boomers to not, as a group, be able to retire as early as others have.[275]

The sheer number of baby boomers by itself means that there will be great increases in the labor force at advanced ages. Figure 20 shows the number of people in three older age brackets in the labor force, along with 2008-based BLS predictions for 2016.[276]

To one way of thinking, high labor force participation for those older should be no real surprise. After all, 65 was the age chosen by German chancellor Otto von Bismarck for a German retirement program, when life expectancy for those born 65 years before, there as well as in America, was about 45.[277] If indexed

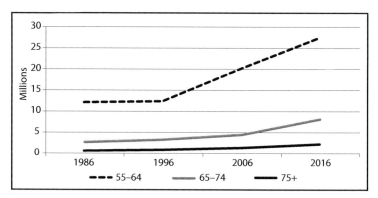

Figure 20: Number Participating in the Labor Force Aged 55+ by Age Group for 1986, 1996, and 2006, and Projected for 2016

to longevity in the same ratio today, using the Centers for Disease Control's 2010 data for those born in 1950,[278] the standard retirement age would now be 98.

With American health and life expectancy ever increasing and trillions removed from American net worth in the late 2000s, both health and financial indicators point to fewer voluntary retirements. The majority of observers have agreed that, because of the 2008–2009

> ## WORK'S NEW AGE PRINCIPLE #5
>
> **Since adoption of retirement at age 65, American life expectancy has increased so much that if indexed in the same way now, retirement would be at age 98.**

recession, baby boomers will want to keep working even longer than they had previously planned.[279] In any case, a huge number of them will remain not retired. As many older Americans will not be able to find work and will stay in or close to the labor force, they will be affected even more than before by Work's New Age.

Structural Unemployment Is a Structurally Weak Idea

Various stories appeared in the summer of 2010 claiming that much of the unemployment problem was due to "structural" causes, or incompatibility between employees and employers. Many jobs, their writers said, were going unfilled since they were located where there were not enough jobseekers or required skills and experience had by few looking for work.[280] Mortimer P. Zuckerman claimed in 2010 that there was "a gross mismatch of available skills and demonstrable needs."[281] Minneapolis Federal Reserve Bank president Narayana Kocherlakota cited a 30% rise in the number of job openings from July 2009 to July 2010, at a time when unemployment actually increased,[282] saying that "firms have jobs, but can't find appropriate workers."[283] Former President Bill Clinton echoed that sentiment, blaming high unemployment on workers having the wrong skills.[284]

Geographical structural employment constantly exists to some extent, and the difference in jobless rates between the best- and worst-faring states increased from 4% to 5% between 2007 and 2010.[285] As of November 2010, there were much vaster differences in available jobs between cities. For example, Washington, San Jose, and New York City had one officially unemployed person per posted job opening, whereas Los Angeles and Miami had six and seven, respectively.[286] Joblessness has been made worse by housing price decreases, causing problems with selling homes and moving.[287] According to Betsey Stevenson, chief economist at the U.S. Department of Labor, as well as by Mortimer P. Zuckerman and *Newsweek* deputy editor Rana Foroohar, those who owe more on their mortgages than their houses can be sold for are much less likely to move to other cities for new employment.[288]

There are problems, however, with the idea of structural employment being unusually critical. As economist Robert J. Samuelson pointed out, housing starts fell from 1.9 million to 600,000 from 2006 to 2010, and new car sales those years, from 17 million to 11.5 million. How, he asked, could those drops not cause a decrease in the number of construction workers and car salesmen?[289] Paul Krugman pointed out that if structural unemployment were a major factor, there would be pockets of high labor demand either geographically or within certain industries,[290] an argument also made by Betsey Stevenson.[291] Krugman also stated that high unemployment boiled down to nothing more than low labor demand,[292] and he cited a 2010 National Federation of Independent Business study showing that employers saw labor-quality problems at an all-time low.[293]

As industries as well as localities evolve, there will always be some structural unemployment.[294] Even in bad times, there will be some unfillable positions. In fact, a 2010 study showed 14% of companies struggling to find people they considered appropriate,[295] and another suggested that the disparity could be responsible for up to one-third of American unemployment.[296] However, the White House's Council of Economic Advisors determined that "job lock" caused by decreased mobility explained only a small fraction of Great Recession job losses.[297] In an era where work is often short-term or otherwise ends quickly, it is clear why those who could get it might not be willing to relocate. In any event, to see that structural employment is only a small factor, all we must do is look at the total number of jobs and job-seekers. According to the Economic Policy Institute in 2010, even if every opening were filled by those counted as unemployed, 80% of the latter would have stayed that way,[298] resulting in an unemployment rate of about 8%, the same number of underemployed and others wanting to work and, since all available ones were taken, no job openings at all. Given those numbers, it is hard to say that the wagging tail of workers and employers misfitting explains the dog of Work's New Age.

Is Anyone Getting Hired for That Advertised Job?

In the year from middle 2009 to middle 2010, posted work opportunities increased 26%, with no increase in actual hiring.[299] When assessing how many positions are available, is a job opening just a job opening? Not really. If we measure the number of employees added by the number of vacancies, whether advertised or not, we can be misled. Twice in my project management career, in 2002 and 2005, I lost a permanent information technology (IT) position and was seeking a replacement. I used a variety of contacts and techniques, one that most basic of modern work searches, the online classified. The number of job ads was much the same in 2002 and 2005, yet in 2002 they were more productive—a similar number of submissions precipitated more return calls, more interviews, and a much quicker accepted offer. Why?

> **WORK'S NEW AGE PRINCIPLE #6**
>
> **Job ads no longer mean job hiring.**

The reason was that the open 2002 positions were filled more quickly. As a result, when I checked the sites then, a higher percentage of ads were truly new, for openings not previously advertised. That year, there were about 30 IT project management job ads at any given time for the Orlando area, and when I logged in twice a week, about 40% of them were new to me. That meant 12 unique opportunities per online visit multiplied by about 100 visits a year, for about 1,200 distinct positions. In 2005, there may also have been about 30 pertinent jobs at a time, but only 20% were first-timers, dropping the annual number to 600, yet one who saw only the snapshot of 30 might have thought Orlando opportunities for IT project managers were just as good. My 2002 and 2005 experience also showed that unadvertised positions, those communicated through personal contacts and other word of mouth means, were also filled more slowly, often much more so. In 2008 hiring was even more sluggish, to the point where, at bimonthly Project Management Institute Central Florida Chapter meetings, many attendees would discuss openings advertised for a long time and mention that they had applied for them weeks or even months before.

It is no secret to anyone else looking for work at multiple times over the past decade that job requirements have also become more specific. For employers, what was in 2002 an effort to canvass friends, Romans, and countrymen to fill a needed spot became in 2005 a search for someone with more particular credentials. As another consistent difference between my searches of 2002 and 2005, and again between 2005 and 2008, job ads went from one to two to three paragraphs of required qualifications, or from ten to fifteen to twenty bullet points. Did this pattern hold for other fields and geographical areas also? Some say it did. Robert J. Samuelson wrote that as the economy loses strength, employers "become more picky and cautious" and will hold off on adding workers even after advertising if their business hasn't improved, or they will only hire the very best candidates.[300] As journalist Megan McArdle put it, "Programmer jobs that once demanded anyone with a pulse and a C++ manual now require that you also have at least three years of experience designing websites for a fast food multinational, speak fluent Tajik, and be proficient in hacky sack."[301] As well, specific knowledge or experience sets in job listings that were once wishes may now be firm requirements. Companies' willingness to train incoming employees has also dropped precipitously, so narrowly-defined experience, even if easily acquired on the job, is now required more than before.[302] Combined with a growing trend of employers using a variety of techniques to identify and reject candidates with potentially expensive health problems,[303] not hiring anyone for open positions has become more common. Accordingly, we can take job ads as evidence of employment activity no longer.

Globalization Keeps Pounding On

Globalization, which can be defined as freer cross-border trade along with development of related economic systems,[304] has advanced steadily since 1973. Before then, in the Winning by Default Years, other countries had much less to offer. Japan had progressed from the 1950s when, quaintly enough, "Made in Japan" usually meant a cheap toy, something ephemeral, or something of poor quality, to producing good electronics and the first exported Toyotas, and Germany had radios, Volkswagens, and sophisticated tools, but there was little idea of free, reasonably even trade between America and other countries. With the oil crisis and Deng Xiaoping's ascent, globalization was out of the gate. Soon would follow the 1980s, when many preferred foreign cars, and when South Korea, with a 1970 Gross National Product the size of Afghanistan's, hosted a successful Olympics. In the 1990s, computer connectivity became the office norm, and formerly poor countries such as Malaysia and Taiwan were producing most of America's televisions and videocassette recorders. Goods from China, which, in the wake of Japan's near-depression and stock market crash, had replaced it as the country Americans most feared economically, began to dominate many areas, and clothing began to claim manufacture in the likes of Thailand and Bangladesh. In 2005, Thomas Friedman published the first edition of globalization's bible, *The World Is Flat*, and debates over its merit, which had been around at least since the first American bought an imported car, got louder and louder.

There is no doubt that the goods and services globalization has provided, through lower prices, innovation, variety, and often higher quality, have greatly benefited American consumers. Former Wall Street CEO Henry M. Paulson said in 2006 that as it fostered competition, globalization was good for America.[305] One clear effect it also has, though, is to facilitate American employers replacing local workers with less expensive foreign ones,[306] to whom American wages, even minimum ones, might seem sky high.[307] For example, the average cost of Bangalore, India, call center operators with six months' experience in the mid-2000s, including all benefits, was $600 to $700 per month.[308] Recessions in particular can give companies cause to cut expenses by exporting jobs,[309] as when firms then eliminate American positions, they may rebuild their workforces overseas instead.[310] Concerns about globalization's effect on employment go back long before presidential candidate Ross Perot's 1992 comment that he expected to hear "a giant sucking sound" as jobs moved from the United States to Mexico.[311]

When companies are able to both manufacture and sell products overseas, they can cut wages and workforces in the United States even more.[312] Progressing from a prototype to mass manufacturing is known as scaling up, and with widely distributed products can involve hiring thousands of workers.[313] For some years, scaling up has been overwhelmingly done in other countries, especially in computer-related industries; in fact, as of 2010, 166,000 people in America worked for companies making them, fewer than when computer assembly started in the United States in 1975.[314] Over all, though manufacturing positions have been moving abroad for decades, the departure of more sophisticated white-collar jobs made possible by higher levels of education in countries such as China and Brazil[315] is more recent.[316] Businesses will often prefer to keep service positions in the same countries as the manufacturing ones, resulting in what has been called "network outsourcing."[317]

So how good are other people now at replacing American employees? The International Monetary Fund determined in 2007 that the number of workers available for similar tasks worldwide had increased fourfold since 1980.[318] A 2009 study found that 71% of American employees were endangered by falling demand for their services, a rising supply of those able to perform them, or both.[319] Princeton professor Alan Blinder predicted a loss of 40 million more American white-collar jobs over the next few decades to globalization alone.[320] Foreign workers are becoming increasingly able; as Rana Foroohar put it, about the company that prepared a pertinent study, "Even million-dollar-a-year McKinsey consultants should be worried; how much longer will it be before $200,000-a-year partners at India's Infosys eat their lunch?"[321]

A third type of job that may soon be sent overseas in large number is manual and non-repetitive.[322] Using a video screen and appropriate controls, lower-paid workers elsewhere could control robots in American workplaces. This technology, the same as that employed in the Korean classrooms mentioned before, is already used in American law enforcement and in the American armed services.[323] The more fortunate others not in any of these groups, Thomas Friedman called "untouchables," vulnerable to neither automation nor globalization.[324]

If a strong dollar makes it more attractive for companies to move jobs out of America, could a weaker dollar help bring them back? Economists disagree.[325] On one side, Gary C. Hufbauer estimated that his forecasted 10% dollar-value drop would increase American exports by $100 billion and create 500,000 American jobs,[326] the increased sales abroad generating more positions when the exporting companies need more goods and services themselves.[327] Cheaper dollars also appeal to foreign tourists, whose American purchases are also the equivalent of exports. On the other, a weaker dollar clearly cannot help when all aspects of a company's manufacturing are done overseas, since it is then no factor, and when components are purchased overseas and assembled stateside, a lower dollar can actually raise costs.[328]

Over all, it is hard to quantify the effects of currency-value changes, as other factors intertwine with them. For example, from 2001 to 2010, though the dollar dropped 31% against a group of top world currencies while exports grew 45%, American manufacturing jobs fell 29%, from 16.4 million to 11.7 million.[329] That may support Martin Ford's contention that jobs moving to cheaper-labor countries is actually a forerunner to automation.[330]

Globalization has been wonderful in many ways, and we should not want to stop it, even if we could. Yet Jeremy Rifkin called globalization and automation the "twin forces" likely to cause massive future unemployment.[331] Clearly, the employment effects of globalization, whether or not preliminary to automation, have been one of the strongest causes of Work's New Age. From the standpoint of American workers, globalization and automation look much the same—jobs disappear, and the goods and services keep coming.[332]

> **WORK'S NEW AGE PRINCIPLE #7**
>
> America now has excess capacity—in workers.

Upshot: The Forecast Calls for Fewer and Fewer Jobs

Businesses often discharge people even when that offers only doubtful advantages. Two studies found companies announcing layoffs from 1979 to 1998 had decreasing stock values. Other research concluded that firms cutting workers from 1977 to 1987 had no productivity gain compared with others, as sales *per employee* actually declined in many cases.[333] Further studies found no connection between downsizing and profitability,[334] and layoffs failed to consistently cut costs either.[335] Additionally, companies shedding workers often get rehiring costs, litigation, sabotage, and workplace violence,[336] and in one inquiry, 88% had overall morale drops.[337] Yet downsizings and other layoffs, that word having changed around 1996 from something temporary to something permanent, are still very much a part of the American business landscape.[338]

Vastly more Americans want to work than can be hired, and the gap will only get larger. As Martin Ford said, "The skills and capabilities of many experienced workers are simply no longer demanded by the future."[339] It has also been a long time since people could easily obtain low-level "survival jobs" for which they were overqualified to tide themselves over. And in early 2010, even President Barack Obama recognized that the American government could help little with job creation.[340]

The United States now has excess capacity—in workers.[341] So what is happening in America when, as Hannah Arendt wrote, "the work society runs out of work?"[342] What effects have we had, and what effects will we see soon? Chapter 3 will tell.

Chapter 3:

The Effects, So Far and Soon

An individual's feelings of low self-efficacy grow out of experiences involving unstable work and low income and are reinforced or strengthened by the similar feelings and views of others who share the conditions and culture of the neighborhood. —William Julius Wilson[343]

Don Peck, deputy managing editor of *The Atlantic*, called nontransitional unemployment "a pestilence that slowly eats away at people, families, and if it spreads widely enough, the fabric of society," and added that the effects of widespread joblessness would take a long time to appear and would last a long time.[344] Beyond those strong and valid observations, how has the shortage of jobs affected Americans?

It's Not 21 to 65 Anymore

In 1945, World War II ended and American soldiers came home. They reunited with their families. They started having baby boom babies. Their pent-up need for goods and services, shared by those who had stayed home and gone without, made the Winning by Default Years the greatest economic explosion in American history. As a result, those who did not go to college on the G.I. Bill went to work, their labor in great demand.

By the early 1950s, the boom had caused clear social effects. Wedding ages dropped. Those who married started families, and the men went to work. Labor in demand meant labor provided. Typical career ages, most would have agreed, were 21 to 65. Fifty years later, by the early 2000s, considerable changes had happened. The economy was good, but with downsizings for numerous people and early full retirement for many more, most weren't working as long. The decade before, journalist Gail Sheehy had published *New Passages* and declared the "gold watch" or retirement stage to begin at age 55.[345] Many, if not most, did not start their first career jobs until around 30. A few years later, professor Aage B. Sørensen said that between beginning work later, ending it earlier, and higher life expectancy, "the needed middle part becomes smaller as the useless parts become larger."[346] Those working in lean production as core workers usually took more time to start their careers and ended them before previous generations did,[347] with their income dropping significantly as a group around age 50.[348] As time went on, more and more people retired at younger ages.

Now, as we will see below, few permanently start full-time work before age 30, and retirement from careers, if anything, is ever earlier. What was a 44-year range only 60 years ago is now often 30 to 50, less than half that length. Let's have a look at what's now beyond both ends of that range.

Full Adulthood's Taking Longer

Over the past few decades, something different has been happening with America's younger adults. As Don Peck wrote, "The 20s have become a sort of netherworld between adolescence and adulthood."[349] Psychologist Jeffrey Arnett agreed, named the stage "emerging adulthood"[350] and described people he considered neither adolescents nor adults as characterized by unsteadiness, self-focus, options assessment, identity exploration, and their own perceptions of being between adolescence and adulthood,[351] if not something closer to wandering or struggling.[352]

The answer is: "Later." The question is: "When are young Americans getting married? As of the 1950s, half of women wedded by 20 and more than half of men by 23.[353] In fact,

Americans born from 1920 to 1945 married earlier, on average, than any other age group in the 20ᵗʰ century.[354] Contrary to modern attitudes for most, getting wedded soon after high school or college graduation was considered a mark of achievement for women.[355] As the Winning by Default Years ended, mean marriage ages for men, which had stayed much the same since 1960, started increasing, from 24.0 in 1975 to 24.8, 25.9, and 27.0 in 1980, 1985, and 1990, respectively. For women, the age crept up to 21.9 in 1975, then increased more quickly: 22.7 in 1980, 24.0 in 1985, and 25.0 in 1990.[356] By 2005, average marriage ages were 27.2 for men and 25.1 for women.[357] As of 2009, the median was 28 for men and 26 for women,[358] the highest ever.[359]

The answer is: "Longer." The question is: "How long are young Americans living with their parents?" In economically poor 1940, 63% of Americans aged 18 to 24 lived with their family of origin, but by 1960 the number had dropped to 42%.[360] From 1977 through the 1980s, the trend reversed, and more stayed longer.[361] By 1994, 51% of men and 37% of women 20 to 24 lived with their parents,[362] and in the mid-2000s, 20% of 26-year-olds still did.[363] The differences over time were even clearer when framed more specifically; the share of 25-year-old white men living with their parents, 12% in 1970, increased to about 20% in 2000 and about 25% in 2007.[364] Those who leave home also often come back again to live; in the late 1990s, almost 40% of young adults who had moved out returned for four months or more,[365] and in 2010, the recession alone had caused 10% of those under 35 who had left home to move back in.[366]

> **WORK'S NEW AGE PRINCIPLE #8**
>
> Younger people, especially those under 20, have become less and less likely to work at all.

Another way of looking at indicators of independence is to combine them into one. Taking completion of five tasks—finishing school, moving away from parents, achieving financial independence, getting married, and having a child—as a gauge of being an established adult, 77% of women and 65% of men in 1930 could claim it at age 30,[367] yet of 30-year-olds in 2000, fewer than half of women and about one-third of men had gotten to that point.[368] As a whole, the years after college have become less encumbered with obligations.[369]

So what is the connection between lower employment opportunities, later marriages, more time living with parents, and later independence in general? Although interviews in 1997 with adult children living at home and their parents showed a wide variety of reasons for the decision to stay or leave,[370] some patterns are remarkably strong. American blacks and Hispanics, long associated with higher unemployment rates, have generally left home later than non-Hispanic whites.[371] Younger adults with jobs have tended to move out earlier,[372] whereas those looking for work stayed longer, even more so than those going to college.[373] As long ago as 1995, Gail Sheehy described the share of Americans aged 19 to 25 who could afford their own apartments, to say nothing of houses, as "tiny." It has been a long time since being able to start at a low-level position in a hierarchical company with hopes of working oneself up has been the norm for people out of high school or college.[374] Only half of people aged 18 to 29 had a full-time job of any kind in 2006, which fell to 41% by early 2010.[375] The portion of those 16 to 24 in the labor force dropped from 66% in 2000 to 56% in 2010, a statistic only partially explained by higher college attendance,[376] with 37% of people of the same ages unemployed or not in the labor force at all.[377] The share of those 16 and 17 years old with work experience in the year plunged from 51.8% in 1987 to 28.5% in 2007. For the same years, those aged 18 to 19 fell from 76.6% to 57.3%, 20 to 24 dropped from 85.5% to 76.6%, and 25 to 34 slipped slightly from 85.7% to 84.2%.[378]

Three key factors have had an effect on delayed full adulthood. Birth control is more available and effective than it was in the 1950s, and more common premarital sex has reduced the perceived value of early marriage. Women are entering most professional career fields, with education and work demands incompatible with giving birth, at similar rates to men, and having even first babies at later ages has become far more common. However modest those jobs actually were, opportunities for career positions for young men were much greater in the 1950s and 1960s than before or since. This third reason may be the most important. In particular, one relationship especially clear involving later true adulthood is the link between career job prospects and traditionally-aged college graduates.[379] The 1970s were not all bad recession years, but they may have seemed like it for graduates seeking entry-level career positions as that market segment became flooded. The slackers of the 1990s may have been unemployed in large part to lack of opportunities instead of lack of ambition.[380] With the Great Recession damaging younger workers disproportionately, jobs offered to new college graduates dropped 28% from 2008 to 2010,[381] and for the year ending February 2011, unemployment for graduates younger than 25 years old averaged 9.5%.[382]

Figure 21 shows labor force participation rates among people of different ages and the changes they have had since 1973.[383]

Note that participation for those aged 16 to 19 has gone way down through good economic times and bad, and has also dropped for those 20 to 24, both declines happening when overall labor force participation increased. The rates for people 16 to 19 and 55 to 64, much the same from 1977 to 1991, have since diverged, as have those for 20 to 24 and 25 to 54. If current trends continue, the participation rates for those 20 to 24 and 55 to 64 will converge, as will those for ages 16 to 19 and 65-plus, developments unthinkable only a couple of decades ago.

Attitudes about younger people's independence have shown some conflict. Recent surveys have revealed that most Americans of all ages believe that by age 22 people should be out of school, out of the parents' house, and working.[384] Although even young adults themselves may think they should be on that schedule, 60% of those in one extended study said they often felt not grown up.[385] Research in 2000 showed that only 41% of those 18

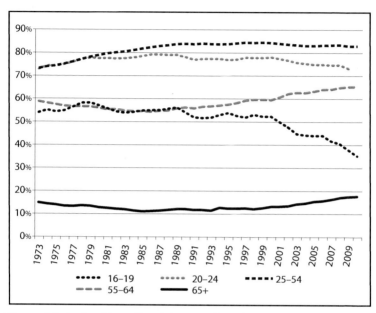

Figure 21: Labor Force Participation Rate by Age, 1973–2010

to 25 years old thought they had clearly reached adulthood, while the share of those aged 26 to 35 was only 68%.[386] Imagine these results in 1943, or even 1970!

Young or emerging adults now constitute a clear economic problem. It is expensive to care for people of any age who are not working, especially when they are in college, which has for decades served a function of warehousing those for whom the job market has little place.[387] Yet ten million more motivated, capable, educated people in their twenties actively seeking full-time work consistent with their education and interests would not be a godsend—it would be a disaster. When journalist Robin Marantz Henig said, "There wouldn't necessarily be jobs for them all,"[388] she understated.

While we cannot see causality from correlation, the relationship seems close between job-market demand, especially for career positions, and independence ages. Overall trends show the post-adolescent phase increasing more in bad times than it has shrunk in good, especially for the past decade or so,[389] its length coinciding remarkably with how much or how little people aged 22 to 30 are needed in the workforce. Jeffrey Arnett wrote that emerging adulthood had "changed the nature of work" for those of that age.[390] Could it be that work or the lack of it has instead changed, or more properly created, emerging adulthood? If so, we can attribute no less than a new stage of life to Work's New Age.

Uncharted Territory: 55-ish with the Career Job Gone

Sue Johnson was born in 1948.[391] She was always smart, having skipped half of two grades in elementary school, but dropped out of the university in favor of a husband, two children, a dog, and a house. In the early 1980s, she put herself through college, majored in computer science, and was soon working as a programmer and project manager. She became an expert at understanding computer users' needs, and was so extraordinarily productive that upon leaving one position, she was replaced by two and a half people. In 1991, she took a similar job with a large Florida telecommunications corporation, where her career flourished for the rest of the decade.

Sue was not concerned when around 2000 her company began bringing in people from India for training and returning them there. She found out, though, that her management planned to use them for outsourcing, as their fully-loaded cost was about one-fifth of that for comparable Americans. In 2002, she was released as part of a group with almost none under 40 and many in their 50s and 60s. The company had to justify the ages of their layoffs, and it may have barely avoided age discrimination liability. She elected to go into business, opening a fitness center, but it failed within a few months. After that, in 2004, she again applied for IT jobs, 300 of them, with no success. Over the next few years, she applied for hundreds of other positions, got nowhere, then moved from Orlando to Milwaukee and did the same, with similar results. Low points she remembers were being turned down for work in a box factory for lack of experience, and not being hired for any job at a bank for which she had designed and programmed their still-in-use deposits system twenty years before.

At 63 and coming off 11 healthy, high-energy years without a good job, Sue is not at all ready to retire. She is now caring for a friend's house in exchange for low rent and is seeking to augment her long-time private pilot's license with certification as a commercial pilot and flight instructor. However, even with her experience, proven ability, and Mensa-level intelligence, she never expects to have a career job again. Her savings are running low, and she is grateful that in less than two years she will be eligible for Medicare.

Sue Johnson, and each of the millions she exemplifies, shows how different work lives have become for many Americans over 50. For most of the 20th century, people worked until they retired at 65. If they changed careers, they often needed to restart lower, but generally as people built up time in one area, they increased or at least maintained their responsibility levels. At the end of many working lives, employees often became less valuable to their organizations than before; postwar business writers such as Robert Townsend and Laurence J. Peter wrote of "mossbacks" who were "retired in place," and of people being promoted until they rose to "the level of their incompetence."[392] Since the Winning by Default Years ended, though, that pattern became rarer and rarer.

Why? The main reason is that many have been ending their career work sooner. Not only have most people been starting their time with good jobs later, but ending it earlier. Furthermore, once older workers become unemployed, they tend to stay that way longer. The November 2009 mean job-finding time for those 55 and older was 36 weeks, compared with 28 for those younger;[393] by March 2010, it was 43 weeks, and 57% had been looking for at least six months.[394] Older workers have been hard hit in total numbers as well; those at least 55 and officially unemployed jumped from 490,000 to 2,114,000, or up 331% from 2000 through the end of 2009.[395]

When those laid off late in their careers get back to work, even if in the same field, they now usually restart with less responsibility and lower pay. According to one study ending in 2009, 63% of those aged 55 or more and discharged in the previous year applied for new positions at lower levels.[396] Another survey showed that about 25% of line and human resource managers involved in hiring had received applications for entry-level jobs from those over 50. Of baby boomers finding work after layoffs, half found it at diminished wages.[397] A 2009 New York City job fair, which over ten years and ten cities had never had more than 2,000 attendees, attracted 5,000 people, mostly middle-aged. Sixteen job-seeking baby boomers there described as "highly motivated" were re-interviewed a year later, with findings that eight were unemployed or working nearly minimum-wage, part-time jobs, seven had full-time jobs paying less than before, and only one had found a position with more money.[398]

So how about older workers unable to find jobs simply retiring? Economists at Wellesley College estimated in early 2010 that 378,000 would take that step through 2015 for poor job availability alone. In the 2009 fiscal year, the Social Security Administration expected a 15% increase in benefit applications but received 21%. Those collecting early could instead gain 7% to 8% per each year they wait, a choice many now see as not viable. In a study at the same time, 64% of those with jobs planned to continue work until 65 or later, but 72% of those now retired, of whom almost half had their jobs end though downsizing or a business closing, ended up leaving the workforce sooner.[399]

How do older people feel about stopping work earlier? For a large number, the answer is "not good at all." Many, especially those in nonphysical but mentally challenging jobs, have kept working not only up to but well past 65 for decades.[400] A 2003 AARP study of the retirement plans of those aged 50 to 70 found that 47% of those not yet retired expected to work into their 70s, 11% more thought they would work until 80, and a further 5% anticipated never retiring as such.[401] Indeed, and in contrast to those under 25, the share of people actually working increased

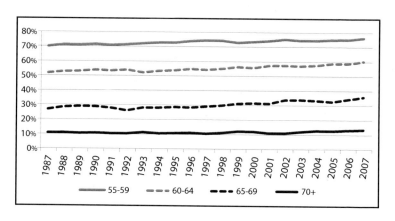

Figure 22: Percent of People 55 and Older with Work Experience during the Year by Age, 1987–2007

from 1987 to 2007 for every large age category over 55, as Figure 22 shows.[402]

More recent stories and research have shown many past 50 worried about never working again, yet as of April 2010, more than one-third of those not retired still planned to continue past 65.[403] In a 2008 study from New York's Families and Work Institute, also before the Great Recession's onset, when people over 50 were asked why they wanted to work later, 53% said they wanted money for a better eventual retirement, the highest of any motive.[404] A 2010 study also found that of people 60 and over postponing retirement, the most common reason was financial.[405]

So why, even with precipitous declines in the value of housing, in many savings plan balances, and in many other investments since then, are many people now declaring themselves retired and applying for early Social Security? The answer is simple. The jobs aren't there, and few think they will be soon. Yet as for retirement, what social policy researcher Peter Townsend wrote in 1963 may still be valid:

> Retirement is a tremendous blow to the man.
> It completely alters his life, lowers his prestige,

> thrusts him into poverty or near poverty, cuts
> him off from the friendships and associations
> formed at work, and leaves him with few oppor-
> tunities of occupying his time.[406]

What will people aged over 50 with employment prospects dampened by Work's New Age—but with financial obligations, health care needs if they are not eligible for Medicare, and vitality better than those ten to twenty years younger in the previous century—do with themselves? A December 2010 Rutgers study revealed that many in that age range will constitute a new group, those "involuntarily retired," with more than 25% expecting to stop trying to work earlier than they would have preferred.[407] Some may start businesses, as in 2009 one-fifth of those 50 and over changing careers became self-employed[408] and people aged 55 to 64 were found to be more likely than those in any other group to be entrepreneurially active,[409] yet very small and unprofitable business efforts, as we will see, distort those numbers. In all, baby boomers over the next few decades will be more interested than previous generations at that age were in working, and will be far more numerous, yet may have few opportunities. In that case, they will function for labor purposes as younger people—all dressed up and no place to go.

The Weight Rooms of Working, and Missing Out on Them

As we have seen, not only has unemployment increased but the share of those looking for work for a long time has gone up even more. After lengthy layoffs, what do their job prospects look like? Bill James, a baseball author, has written 26 books in the field and was cited in the 2006 TIME 100 as one of the world's influential people.[410] In an essay in his *Baseball Abstract 1988*, he described why National Football League players, then on strike and being substituted for by others, could not maintain their status much longer:

In the first week of replacement-level games, there were some players who played so well that they established pretty clearly that they should have been there all along. As each week passes, another one or two players per team is going to establish that he is better than one of the 45 guys who isn't there. Further, as each week passes the players who are playing, competing as they are at the best level of football available, benefiting from the level of training, benefiting from the coaching and the weight rooms, benefiting from the experience, get a little bit better—while the players who aren't playing, week after week, get a little bit worse, their skills deteriorating from age…until after a period of time that fine line that distinguished those who were in from those who were out just disappears.

Suppose that the players were to stay on strike for, let us say, two years. At the end of that time, if the Union were to say "'OK, we give up, go back to work," there wouldn't be any jobs for them to go back to, simply because they would, for the most part, no longer be good enough to play.[411]

The same sentiment has since been published by Robert J. Samuelson, who noted that "people lose workplace contacts; some skills atrophy or vanish, because they were tied to a specific company or a fading technology,"[412] and by Paul Krugman, who said, "Every year that goes by with extremely high unemployment increases the chance that many of the long-term unemployed will never come back to the work force."[413] Even a solid economic recovery will not help many who have been out a long time,[414] and they must consider the possibility that their working days are over.[415] In the meantime, as of late 2010, those unemployed for more than one year had an 8.7% chance of finding a job in the next month, compared with 30.7% for those out of work fewer than five weeks.[416]

The problems with being jobless are especially severe for those in technical fields, where the evolution and replacement of, say, computer languages, methodologies, and even software versions provide clear knowledge differences between those who have and have not been in offices where technology is generally newer and better than in homes. With hardware product names and software release numbers often included on résumés, the gap between those who have been recently working in information technology and those who have not becomes pronounced with the first job application. Accordingly, the problem of people's work qualifications deteriorating is very real. What will happen when more and more people are frozen out of careers they once had? What will happen when more and more people perceive they can't get hired at all?

The American Rasta Class

Paul Krugman maintained that where there is especially high long-term unemployment, there is a risk of those involved becoming a permanent, non-working underclass,[417] a concern voiced by Jeremy Rifkin, who said long before that it would form an environment ripe for civil disorder,[418] and Bob Herbert, who called it "a recipe for societal destabilization."[419] Economist and historian Zachary Karabell spoke in 2009 of "a permanent pool of millions of unemployed in the midst of an economy that is otherwise doing well."[420]

What happens when a whole section of a country is unable to find work? Jamaica has had that experience for decades. The Rastafarians are a religious group defined by their belief in the divinity of the late Ethiopian emperor Haile Selassie.[421] They developed a culture around their principles, which include a well-integrated Afrocentric view of biblical history. In the 1970s, they had average education levels similar to other Jamaicans and higher rates of literacy and reading.[422] They lived close to nature and close to each other.[423] They often wore very long beards and grew their hair, which formed wrapped-together strands called dreadlocks,[424] in similar fashion. They smoked *ganja* (marijuana) in large quantities as a sacrament, referred to the pipe as a chalice, prayed each time they started to smoke, and believed it aided both thinking and social ties.[425]

So how could such habits as growing hair extremely long and frequently smoking marijuana be compatible with typical working lives? The answer is they weren't. Few Rastafarians had jobs, and in the 1970s they were joined by discouraged high school and college students who did not think conditions in Jamaica would improve.[426] In 1977, overall Jamaican unemployment, no doubt higher in poorer regions, was 17% for men and 30% for women.[427] The problem of entire neighborhoods filled with those hopeless about finding work is hardly confined to less developed countries, but it was true in France even during the relatively economically strong 1990s.[428] Did Jamaican joblessness influence the adoption of cultural practices maladaptive for work, or did only the practices themselves hinder employment? We do not know, but with such a well-developed culture that would go poorly with most jobs, the former seems to have merit.

In America, ghetto areas have been known for work shortages for close to a century, but in recent years, the problem has become far worse. In 1976 I drove a taxi in Milwaukee, then well known for its high level of de facto segregation but with relatively low unemployment and, at the time, a reputation for having the lowest crime rate of any American city around its size. The "inner city" on the North Side, where I frequently picked up and dropped off customers, was populated mainly by blacks and Germans. Although its neighborhoods were the poorest in the county, the houses overwhelmingly looked structurally sound and well maintained, their business districts bustled with activity from a full contingent of stores, and there were jobs. One day I picked up a boy about ten years old from an inner-city house. We drove past A.O. Smith, then a large maker of automobile frames, and he said, "My daddy works there." That was nothing unusual at the time—not only did most children, even those from the poorest places, have fathers, but the fathers had jobs. While A.O. Smith had mostly hard, physical positions that did not pay high wages, they provided health insurance, vacations, a pension, and enough money to support, though modestly, a family. If you worked at A.O. Smith and came back to a spouse and children, you were a provider, a contributor, most likely doing the job at home as well as in the factory.

So what has happened since then? Milwaukee's connection with the automobile industry went from good to bad in the 1980s. Many jobs were lost. The city's crime rate advanced to about average in both property and violent crimes for cities about its size,[429] with the problems concentrated in the North Side inner city.[430] Its ten largest employers have changed from all industrial in 1970 to four health care, two retailing, and one each banking, insurance, utility, and printing,[431] most of which have lower median inflation-adjusted wage levels. And A.O. Smith, while still a substantial company with $2 billion in annual sales, has long since closed its Milwaukee factory, with its main products, hot water heaters, made now in Ashland City, Tennessee and Nanjing, China.[432] Similar problems to Milwaukee's, also occurring after widespread job losses, were documented in a 2009 study of two Philadelphia neighborhoods.[433]

What is happening now is that, in the words of Harvard sociologist William Julius Wilson, "For the first time in the twentieth century most adults in many inner-city ghetto neighborhoods are not working in a typical week."[434] When there are *employment* rates such as the 37% and even 23% of adults documented for two Chicago inner-city neighborhoods, the social fabric deteriorates,[435] especially severely when many of the jobless are unmarried men.[436] When legitimate sources of income become scarce, more people resort to illegal ones, particularly selling drugs.[437] With drugs come more and more guns, not kept quietly as in other areas but often brandished by teenagers who, with poorer judgment anyway and often under the influence of the drugs, "are tempted to solve temporary problems in

a very permanent fashion."[438] Most businesses disappear; in Chicago's poor North Lawndale area, which a few decades before
had 67,000 jobs at three departed employers alone, there were in
1986 only one bank and one supermarket but 99 bars and liquor
stores.[439] The people in such places clearly want jobs, as, according to Chicago's Urban Poverty and Family Life Study, 97% of
black ghetto-area respondents considered hard work important
for success.[440] Yet as one respondent, who happened to have a job,
said, it would be good to find work "and not take six months to
do it."[441] Not surprisingly, problems parents have with controlling
teenagers and younger children in such environments cause bad
conditions to perpetuate.[442]

   Is American inner-city culture already akin to the Jamaican
Rastafarians? If not as of the time of the Chicago study above, it
could be now. Once people see no hope, they change their lives
accordingly. If internal reasons alone are insufficient motivation,
then why should human beings make sacrifices for opportunities
that will not be forthcoming? Poor does not mean stupid.

   Could the loss of jobs, especially among men, cause many
more American areas to have inner-city characteristics?[443] In late
2009, the national unemployment rate for black males aged 16 to
19 was 57%, way up from 34% only two years before.[444] Many
problems similar to those in black inner cities are appearing in
largely white rural, town, and small city areas with high unemployment.[445] According to journalist Gabor Steingart in 2008, a
new American underclass is already emerging, with most intel-
lectually deteriorating, smoking, drinking excessively, eating
unhealthy foods, and spending vast hours watching television.[446]
Largely uneducated and politically apathetic, they, as Steingart
put it, "have already given up on themselves." He claimed it was
not random that the class's coalescence happened at the same
time as extensive job losses, which he blamed for its members'
social and personal unraveling.[447]

   One more situation not only indicates societal decay but
serves to remove people from the labor force in its own right:
America's increasing prison population. Between 1980 and

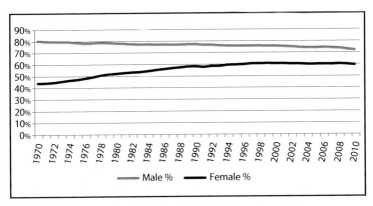

Figure 23: Percentage in Labor Force by Sex, Ages 16+,
    1970–2010

1996, the number of inmates tripled, and it reached 1.6 million by 2000.[448] If this jump had not occurred, there might be another million largely young people in the labor force. Though their status is different, those in prison are another group for whom the labor market has little place; we would have to look quite hard to find employers complaining that they cannot find enough young, poor, inner-city-dwelling workers because so many are incarcerated.

William Julius Wilson said in 2010 that very high unemployment in neighborhoods would automatically damage them socially and that "we're going to see some horror stories."[449] That, around the country in areas of all ethnicities, is a danger we face in Work's New Age.

The Reverse Brain Drain

The expression "brain drain" is not new to Americans. Throughout the 20th century, it meant one thing: smart, educated, often highly trained foreigners were moving to the United States to become more prosperous than they could be back home. If it were possible, why shouldn't Indian doctors, Russian rocket scientists, or Iraqi professors move here for American lifestyles and incomes? Especially in the postwar years, the brain drain amounted to a great gift to the United States and helped cement America's top industrial and intellectual position worldwide. Yet while beneficial to the people involved, it was sadly detrimental to their original countries; how could Nigeria, Indonesia, or Bolivia develop if its best minds were siphoned off?

More recently, though, brains have been draining the other way. The opposite term, "reverse brain drain," has been in use since at least 2004 and can mean different things. One sense often appearing in the press is the tendency of American-educated foreigners to return to their home countries instead of staying in the United States. A second meaning is a sort of brain swap, in which American companies outsource white-collar and professional work overseas; the result is former stateside jobs, generally good ones such as in computer programming, product design, and technical management,[450] being replaced by those elsewhere.

A third sense is the most ominous, and it may be growing faster than the other two. It is the departure of intelligent, well-educated and -trained United States citizens themselves, in the same sense as the original brain drain a generation or two before. Many are entrepreneurs, teachers, or those with specific technical abilities, exactly those workers frequently mentioned as desirable, sought-after, and insufficient in quantity in America. As well, new expatriates are most commonly not those near or in retirement but of ages 25 to 34,[451] meaning that their contributions are relative bargains in terms of physical and mental energy, productivity, salaries and health insurance costs.

Losing these people is unattractive, but if there aren't enough jobs in the United States, many will go to where they think they can find them. That is another reality of Work's New Age.

Havoc between Men and Women

In the 1930s, sociologist Mirra Komarovsky wrote about the effect of Great Depression joblessness on family life. She concluded that unemployed men's marriages deteriorated, with less socializing, less sex, and lowered respect from their wives.[452]

Much more recently, Don Peck found that men who lost their jobs usually had more conflict in their marriages. Recently-unemployed men described their identities weakening and their states of isolation.[453] Many women still think of men without jobs as worthless, and men's pictures of who they are tend to be defined by their work, much more so than for women, so both partners feel great discomfort when the man becomes unemployed.[454] The Great Recession job losses, with men receiving 6 million and 75% of them and resulting in more than half of workers as of 2010 being women,[455] may challenge many marriages, when men have or at least perceive they have little other than income to contribute.[456] As more women have joined the labor force, shown in Figure 23,[457] many may already have shown, through their matrimonial decisions, that men have insufficient value for them, as the share of women aged 30 to 44 who were married dropped from 84% in 1970 to 60% in 2010.[458]

December 2010 unemployment rates were 9.5% for men and 8.5% for women, a gap actually much wider in late 2009.[459] Work may shift even more to women, as 13 of 15 job categories expected to add the most workers in the 2010s have men in the minority. In few current American jobs do men's generally greater size and strength play a role, but women's often superior social and communication skills are valuable in many. According to Hanna Rosin, senior editor at *The Atlantic*, office work has moved from accommodating women to being molded further by them. Many of the largest-growing jobs involve nurturing, which men are able to do but historically have not succeeded at as well as women, who are now also receiving 60% of B.A. and master's degrees and about half of those in law and medicine.[460] If it is true, as Rick Newman put it, that "women are now getting ahead because men aren't,"[461] we could see some real social problems. Great relative progress for women, without significant social adjustments by both sexes, may come at the cost of large numbers of men feeling obsolete,[462] another hazardous possibility of Work's New Age.

Sick Income, Sick Body

Much research points to worsening health during unemployment.[463] One study showed that between 1970 and 1990, men aged 40 to 60 were significantly more likely to die after losing their jobs, even after getting new ones. Average lifespans, 18 months less than those who had experienced no unemployment, were shortest among workers who had been laid off at younger ages.[464] Those jobless at length before they turned 30, without regard to previous history, had high rates of depression and were more likely than most to become middle-aged binge drinkers, problems which often continued even when they got work.[465]

Another result of both unemployment and the health problems that often follow it is withdrawal from community activity.[466] Robert P. Putnam, political scientist and *Bowling Alone* author, said some civic disengagement remained even after unemployed people found jobs.[467] Other factors that subtract a year and a half from life expectancy are often treated more seriously, as epidemics. Could a shortage of work constitute the same?

Upshot: New Age for Social Patterns as Well

Jobs are valuable to people not only for incomes, but for their sense of purpose, their instilling of hope for personal or professional improvement, and as motivators for education.[468] Don Peck called the unemployment crisis "a slow-motion social catastrophe" that could make America weaker for generations and said we were obligated to do all we could to "stop it now."[469] How can we deal with it? In Part II, I evaluate possible courses of action.

Part II: The Solutions

Chapter 4:
What Do the Papers Say?

*Generating new jobs for a growing population is a
challenge to the left, right, and center of all our political parties and their entrenched positions on economic
issues.* —Mortimer P. Zuckerman[470]

Twenty-Eight Suggestions

I found nine articles published between October 2009
and September 2010 on how to increase employment. One
commentary was written by applied economist Steven J.
Davis, one by Robert J. Samuelson, one by associate editor
Derek Thompson of *The Atlantic*, two by Rick Newman, one
by business writer Nancy Cook, one by former Secretary of
Labor Robert B. Reich, and one by the team of *24/7 Wall St.*
editors, Douglas A. McIntyre, Michael B. Sauter, and Ashley
C. Allen. The ninth was presented by *The New York Times*
editorial staff and included opinions from economists Tyler
Cowen, James K. Galbraith, Heather Boushey, Jeffrey A.
Miron, and Mark Thoma. As well as in *The Times*'s Room for
Debate blog, they appeared in *Forbes, The Washington Post,
The Atlantic*, and *U.S. News & World Report*. The writers' eco-
nomic and political views varied considerably—conservative,

liberal, free-market capitalist, and Keynesian. After some similar ideas were combined, the 13 respondents, counting co-authors McIntyre, Sauter, and Allen as one, offered a total of 28 specific, materially different governmental suggestions.

Direct federal payments to states were mentioned three times.[471] Four named tax cuts or disbursements to companies for hiring.[472] Loans or tax cuts for small businesses in particular were mentioned by three more.[473] One suggested an accelerated investment tax credit,[474] and another recommended reducing taxes on interest, dividends, and capital gains.[475] One proposed tax cuts for weatherizing houses. Three offered changes to the payroll tax: reductions, holidays, or changes to its income distribution.[476] One suggested tax deferrals for companies in financial trouble. Two proposed tax benefits for employers reducing hours or offering job sharing.[477] Allowing the Bush-era tax cuts to lapse was mentioned once,[478] and another recommended making income tax rates more progressive,[479] but a third wanted the Bush tax cuts to be permanent.[480] One proposed contributing toward shipping of exports.[481]

Worker retraining was mentioned once, and two articles proposed a national wage insurance system to pay if workers lost some or all of what they previously earned.[482] One suggested extending unemployment benefits to help the economy in general.[483] One respondent recommended infrastructure and Works Progress Administration (WPA)-style, federally-funded construction efforts.[484]

Two writers said it would be valuable to pay down the national deficit.[485] On the other side, two proposed raising government spending in general.[486] Three suggested reducing or eliminating the federal minimum wage.[487] One respondent recommended lowering the Medicare entitlement age and removing the Social Security early retirement penalty.[488] Taking forceful action with regard to European economic problems appeared once,[489] as did doing the same with China and their economic policies.[490]

Creating a task force to cut business reporting requirements was mentioned once.[491] One proposed ending various health insurance mandates, and the same writer suggested removing labor union organizing and facilitating the Employee Free Choice Act.[492] Another wanted to cut federal protection for unions.[493]

Figure 24 recaps the above suggestions. I have chosen nine of the ideas, along with others, to discuss further in the next three chapters. Six more relate to subsequent material. On the other 13 are brief comments from a Work's New Age perspective.

Suggestion	Comments
Accelerate the investment tax credit	Could help in some situations.
Continue the Bush-era tax cuts	Has since happened, with results not yet known.
Contribute toward export shipping	Could help, but would be better to subsidize jobs instead. See Chapter 7.
Cut business reporting requirements	A good idea, but would that encourage already-profitable businesses to hire more?
Cut federal union protection	Worsening the status of private-sector unions, which are becoming less and less important anyway and are still emotionally valuable to many, would be a poor choice.
Cut taxes for weatherizing houses	One of many possible small ideas that could be evaluated.
Cut taxes or make payments to businesses for hiring	See Chapter 7.
Defer taxes for companies in financial trouble	Would help.
End the Bush-era tax cuts	The tax cuts have since been renewed.
End the Employee Free Choice Act	See "Cut federal union protection."
End various health-insurance mandates	See Chapter 7.
Extend unemployment benefits	See Chapter 7.
Implement a national wage insurance system	Would benefit many people but would neither help those already jobless nor with time limits solve the problem of ever-lengthening unemployment. See Chapters 7 and 8 for related ideas.

Implement tax benefits for reduced hours or job sharing	See Chapter 7.
Implement WPA-style construction programs	See Chapter 7.
Lower the Medicare entitlement age	Expensive, and there could be a better way than Medicare and its "reasonable and customary" allowances, but doing so would end health care fear. See Chapter 7 for more.
Lower taxes on interest, dividends, and capital gains	With businesses profitable but not hiring, seems doubtful to cause job creation.
Make federal payments to states	Would help without increasing taxes, if the federal government had the money.
Make income tax more progressive	Could help but would be unworkable over time as rates would have to increase more and more. See Chapter 7 for other tax ideas.
Modify the payroll tax, with cuts, holidays, or changes	Would help.
Pay down the national deficit	Could help in the long run, but can the short run afford it?
Provide loans or tax cuts to small businesses	See Chapter 6.
Raise government spending in general	Some would help, some would not.
Reduce or eliminate the minimum wage	See Chapter 7.
Remove the Social Security early retirement penalty	Would decrease demand for jobs but would increase the entitlement's cost. See Chapter 7 for other ideas.
Retrain more workers	See Chapter 5.
Take action with Chinese economic policies	See Chapter 5.
Take action with European economic problems	What kind of action? See Chapter 5 about protectionism.

Figure 24: Disposition of the 28 Employment-Boosting Suggestions

Chapter 5:

Non-Solutions

There is still a widespread view in the West that China will eventually conform, by a process of natural and inevitable development, to the Western paradigm. This is wishful thinking. —Martin Jacques[494]

Education and Training: One Applicant over Another

To combat unemployment, many observers have suggested retraining workers or getting them more education. Rana Foroohar wrote that better elementary and high schools were necessary for Americans to compete in the global market[495] and later maintained that the solution for unfilled jobs was retraining workers.[496] President Obama said in March 2011 that unemployment improvement would depend on spending more money on education.[497] Mortimer P. Zuckerman held that "millions drawing the dole to sit around should be in training."[498] Betsey Stevenson said more moderately that "there are always workers who could benefit from training,"[499] matched by columnist Liz Wolgemuth recommending it for the discouraged jobless.[500] As of 2010, Stevenson was working two large projects to make the Department of Labor's job retraining programs larger and better.[501]

Efforts to prepare applicants for specific jobs have mixed results. On one side, a Georgia offering that gave workers six weeks of on-the-job training along with as much as $600 for expenses reported thousands of successful placements, with a $12 million welfare savings.[502] Yet Megan McArdle wrote in 2010 that government retraining programs had "a dismal record."[503]

Education and even training are valuable for many purposes, including personal enrichment, but they are not the tools we need to combat widespread joblessness. Good or bad, effective or not effective, justified or not justified, attempts to help individual applicants get work, be they résumé preparation, interview help, technical courses, or even most general education, are not responsive to the overall problem. The issue is that the number of job-seekers is dwarfing the number of available positions. There are other concerns with such efforts as well. Most vocational training prepares people for entry-level jobs, exactly the kind now most flooded with applicants. Not many such programs could have the speed and flexibility to result in people actually getting hired for the few highly specialized positions for which employers honestly want and can't find reasonably qualified candidates, such as experienced users of the currently most sought-after computer technology, even if market demand did not change before the training was completed. Suggesting schooling is ultimately evasive, placing blame either on workers for not being trained for exactly what employers want right now or on the education system, which has its own profound problems. College degrees are now often worthless for getting middle-class-paying jobs,[504] and from 2000 to 2010, average earnings for those with them did not increase.[505] As for competing globally, for which Thomas Friedman, among others advocated more education to contend for worldwide employment,[506] schooling is no help for jobs that have been automated away or even moved to other countries. Who can train anyone to live in America on the $300 to $400 monthly that call center workers earn in India?[507]

Except for filling jobs that would otherwise go empty, which does happen, improving the hireworthiness of specific people who already want work is not a public policy answer. As Paul Krugman put it, "The notion that putting more kids through college can restore the middle-class society we used to have is wishful thinking."[508] The same logic holds for communities out-bidding others for workplaces. Jack may well benefit profession-ally and personally from education or training and even get work with it, but helping Jack get a job that otherwise Jill would have had, or helping Lincoln obtain a factory otherwise slated to be built in Lawrence, accomplishes nothing with the problems of Work's New Age.

Fake Economic Activity Doesn't Help

When is economic activity not economic activity? When it doesn't produce any net gain in prosperity. If I give you a dollar for a product or service, that's a real thing, but when I give you a dollar and you give me a dollar back, it's meaningless. If you give me a dollar for nothing, that isn't economic activity either, only a money transfer. Poker games may be good recreation, and some players can earn income or even a living at them, but economi-cally they are no different from people sitting at tables without cards and giving each other dollar bills. The old example was of people taking in each other's laundry, in which Linda does Lisa's washing for say $10, and Lisa does the same for Linda.

Some of what seem to be business propositions are little better. Making and selling crafts, for most, pays little beyond the cost of the materials, and if those who sell them also like to buy them, they're in effect taking in each other's laundry. Selling per-sonal possessions at garage sales, flea markets, or the likes of eBay can be a useful way to raise money, but it is finite, not profitable (except for those who purposefully buy items to resell and show net profits over and above their car and other expenses), and not a job. Other small business experiences not replacing employ-ment will be presented in the next chapter. Here, though, I will discuss something to which the majority of Americans have been exposed: multilevel marketing (MLM).

Multilevel marketing, also called network marketing, is a system in which participants, called distributors, are paid a per-centage not only of their sales of the company's products but of sales made by distributors they have recruited, sales by distributors <u>those</u> have recruited have recruited,[509] and so on, all of whom form their "downlines." Ever since the first, Nutrilite, was established in 1945, millions of people have joined MLM companies,[510] and tens of millions of others have faced recruitment efforts. As of 1997, such organizations had a combined 5 to 10 million distributors selling $10 billion to $20 billion in products annually, with more of their sales going to other distributors than to outside customers.[511]

Well over half of new multilevel marketing distributors disengage during their first year.[512] Most of those who remain earn little money. As of 1991, the average Amway supplier earned $780 per year before expenses, which would include car, telephone, postage, and various materials. The distributors also personally consumed an average of more than $1,000 in Amway products, of which only 19% over all were used by non-distributors.[513] A 1983 episode of the CBS television program *60 Minutes* presented the Wisconsin attorney general's finding that not even 1% of Amway's 20,000 distributors in that state had as much as $14,000 per year in gross income, and more than half achieved a net loss. To have an ostensible chance of success, enrollees must, in addition to expense money, lay out vast quantities of time at social events[514] and at various meetings, and must also spend time reading and listening to motivational materials. The damage often done to a distributor's social relationships can be considerable, as, according to authors Robert L. Fitzpatrick and Joyce K. Reynolds, "No relationship is outside the MLM sell."[515]

There is a lot of commonality between MLM and outright pyramid schemes. At one South Florida distributor's meeting, in order to achieve annual incomes of at least $100,000, the 500 participants were encouraged to build downlines of 1,000 people.[516] If all succeeded, there would need to be at least 500,000 new enrollees, and that group was among many in Florida alone. Even if all achieved that goal, the additional enrollees, in order to reach that income level themselves, would need to recruit a total of 500 million more—more than half again America's current population. Later realizing these sorts of mathematical facts is probably a reason why, in sharp contrast to those who have tried but failed at other businesses, unsuccessful MLM veterans often say the experience was not worthwhile.[517]

Some MLM distributors do make significant money. As of 1997, the largest Amway one, Dexter Yager, had a $35 million business with his vast downline, but his sales were primarily from motivational products.[518] Some MLM's are valid, emphasize their products and services instead of potential financial gains, and don't represent that one can make a good career in them without hard work.[519] But the microscopic share of people who achieve anything like an after-expenses living income means that MLM efforts are no solution to the problems of Work's New Age. And other illusory economic activity is no better.

Protectionism: Cutting off Our Nose to Spite Our Face

"Comparative advantage" is an economic term for what a person, company, or country has if they can deliver something at a lower percentage of what others can provide it for, in relation to their other products. If it costs Samsung and Toshiba the same amount to make identical laptops but Samsung can produce printers for less than Toshiba charges for similar models, Samsung has a comparative advantage over Toshiba in printers. If it costs Samsung 10% more to make a laptop than Toshiba and it costs Samsung 5% more to make a printer, now Toshiba has a comparative advantage in laptops, but Samsung, strangely enough, has a comparative advantage in printers, since the difference is less. If a factory in rural China can produce a stuffed bear for one-tenth of what an Arkansas plant has to pay and can make a toy car for one-third the amount, the Arkansas plant actually has a comparative advantage in toy

> **WORK'S NEW AGE PRINCIPLE #9**
>
> From the point of view of customers, trading one product for another is the same as taking the resources for the first and making the second with them instead.

cars. When I worked at a pizza restaurant a long time ago, I was clearly the best prep cook and took orders at the counter as well. Although I had not yet encountered the concept of comparative advantage, my manager and I used it to determine that, although I would probably have been the best counter person, it would not be by as much of a margin as I had over others with my prep work, so my working hours would have been better spent doing preps. Likewise, a company president who excels at skills such as keying and filing may hire someone to do them for him, even if his work would be superior.[520]

Comparative advantage can clearly show how trade between two countries, even if one is more efficient at all goods involved, benefits both. For example, suppose Canada can produce deerskin hats for $5 apiece and maple syrup for $10 a gallon, while America requires $30 to make comparable hats and $15 for the same amount of syrup. The reasons could be from the labor force (more skilled syrup or hat makers), natural resources (more deer and more maple trees), capital (more investment in deer or tree farms), technology (better tree-tappers or deer-skinning devices), lower costs, a combination of these, or others. Canada can then produce a deerskin hat and a gallon of maple syrup for $15, while in the United States the pair costs $45. As above, although both items cost less in Canada, which has the comparative advantage in hats, America has the lead in syrup. If Canada agrees to trade a hat to America for a gallon of syrup, the cost for the two items becomes $10 for Canada ($5 for the hat they traded and $5 for the hat they kept), and $30 for the United States ($15 for the gallon of syrup they retained and $15 for the syrup they exchanged), an improvement for both. If any protectionist measures such as tariffs or quotas prevented this trade, each country would pay 50% more for the two items together than they would need if they imported and exported freely.[521] Note that protectionism, in this simple example, does not cause higher prices for products in countries which have comparative advantages in them, but does for goods and services where the advantage is held by others.

There are two ways of getting products such as the deerskin hats above. First, they can be made directly. Second, they can be conjured up indirectly. In the example above, deerskin hats can be "made" by tapping maple trees, boiling the sap, and making maple syrup from it! As *Financial Times* economist Tim Harford pointed out, the direct effect to Americans in the second case is the same as if there were a rather advanced facility that could convert syrup to hats.[522] Protectionism weakens or even eliminates this option.

> **WORK'S NEW AGE PRINCIPLE #10**
>
> **If American workers are too expensive on the world market, then comparative advantage theory says America should produce fewer workers.**

What about exporting but not importing? That would cause problems with money exchanging, as sellers need to obtain their own currency, which must ultimately come from those who have sold to the seller's country. As Tim Harford put it, "Exports pay for imports," and "a 'no imports' policy is also a 'no exports' policy." Similarly, the 1936 Lerner theorem, a classic piece of work on trade, proved that taxes on imports are equivalent to taxes on exports.[523]

Yet protectionism does have beneficiaries.[524] In the case of price subsidies to American sugar producers, the 1998 winners were the owners of sugar farms, who collected a total of $1 billion, whereas the losers were almost all other Americans, who, because of additional market changes the subsidies cost, dropped a total of about $2 billion.[525] Trade barriers may indeed get many people more money, but much of their value may be neutralized by inflationary effects, including fewer goods for sale.[526] Generally, protectionist laws help those in specific groups while damaging everyone else.[527] Likewise, banning products allegedly being "dumped" or sold below cost, which often only means the seller has a comparative advantage,[528] benefits certain American companies and workers but not most Americans.[529]

Protectionism also violates the principle of using resources wisely. With it, people's choices are more limited than they would be with trading partners importing and exporting at more favorable terms.[530] Circumstances of trade will never be equal; for example, as economics professor Russell Roberts pointed out, though few oranges grow in Minnesota, that could be done with greenhouses and other resources, but the chance of such fruit having a comparative advantage over Florida's would be slim indeed.[531] In all, close trading ties help national prosperity, often greatly, and a large majority of economists wholeheartedly support them.[532]

As of 2001, there were thousands of American tariffs and import quotas, so the country could not be called a free trade zone.[533] So what effect does, and will, free trade have on jobs? Historically it has not increased or lowered their number, but it has changed their types.[534] The positions, though, may be better or worse than those previous. So if that pattern stays the same, with free trade we are left with no damage to either job quantity or quality but with the lower-price aspect, which I will discuss later. For now, though, here is a question for you: If other countries have a comparative advantage over the United States on labor, does that mean America needs to stop producing workers? If not, why not? In Chapter 8, I will consider just that.

Crying about China

Since longtime leader Mao Zedong's death in 1976, China's economic progress has been awesome indeed. Although its economy had grown 4% to 5% per year during Mao's 1949–1976 tenure, it averaged 9.5% from 1977 to 2007,[535] doubling its per-capita production during the first ten years,[536] an all-time record for a major economy.[537] Employment and GDP portions from agriculture dropped from 83% and 60%, respectively, in 1952 to 51% and 16% in 2003.[538] In 1994, Chinese-American trade was below $40 billion;[539] between 1993 and 2008, it expanded sixteenfold.[540] From 1990 to 2000, Chinese urban population increased from 25% to 40%, with perhaps 200 million people moving.[541] Per-person income grew from $339 in 1990 to more than $1,000 in 2003[542] and was seven times higher in the late 2000s than thirty years before.[543] As of 2004, an amazing 75% of its GDP came from international trade, compared with no more than 30% for Japan, Brazil, India, or the United States,[544] and no country exported, or exports, more to America.[545] In fact, in the early 2000s Wal-Mart, were it a nation, would have been sixth worldwide in Chinese imports.[546] As of 2006, from 25% to 66% of the world's mobile phones, TV sets, personal digital assistants, car stereos, desktop computers, DVD players, digital cameras, photocopiers, and microwave ovens, along with shoes, toys, and textiles, were made in China.[547] In 2008, it made more cement, coal, and steel than any other country, and its construction in progress, 28 billion square feet in 2005, was five times America's.[548]

As of 2009, China still had an annual growth rate more than 10%.[549] Chinese poverty dropped from almost 55% of the population in 1981 to less than 10% in 2001, with 200 million fewer people in the category, the most successful such reduction in human history.[550] Although China's population has only roughly doubled since the 1960s, movement from the countryside is so great that as of 2008 it had all 20 of the world's quickest-growing cities.[551] Chinese government today could be described as semi-totalitarian; people are free to work, buy and own property, relocate, launch their own businesses, and have some freedom of religion, yet they have sharply limited political rights and cannot access many Internet sites.[552]

China has caused some legitimate concerns about American employment. The country, which exports far more from America than it imports for a trade surplus quickly rising since 1999,[553] has many impediments to free trade other than tariffs.[554] America's need for operating capital may eventually allow China to dictate terms that would help its own position in the world at the expense of that of the United States.[555] In the meantime, many Americans have thought that China's stronger economy has driven its bolder international stance.[556]

In 2006, China had foreign currency assets of $1.81 trillion,[557] almost double second-place Japan's,[558] and more than 60% were believed to be in dollars.[559] China has clearly been storing other currencies as a way of keeping the yuan renminbi[560] weak and therefore its export prices low,[561] though that could also be caused by exchange problems previously described from being export-heavy. The Chinese government has also been encouraging saving to the detriment of consumption as another means to suppress the renminbi's value.[562] Robert Scott of the Economic Policy Institute claimed that if the Chinese currency were to be "properly valued," the country's goods would increase more than 65% in price.[563] In November 2010, leaders of the U.S. House of Representatives stated that if China allowed the value of the renminbi to float, a million American manufacturing positions would be generated.[564] Scott made a similar assertion, but for a million jobs in response to overall currency realignment, including those in Thailand, Indonesia, Korea, Japan, and Switzerland, and that China's currency readjusting would cause the others to be valued more properly.[565] Yet according to Derek Thompson, a higher renminbi wouldn't be enough to move manufacturing back to America, as it has been lost due to globalization in general,[566] and, as Harvard professor Mark Wu explained, further Chinese currency strengthening would be more likely to move jobs to places like Vietnam and Indonesia instead of returning them to the United States.[567]

Early in the 2000s, what Zachary Karabell and historian Niall Ferguson called "Chimerica," the merger of both countries' economies, took hold.[568] Over the past decade, as journalist Fareed Zakaria put it, "The Chinese oversaved, the Americans overconsumed. The system seemed to balance out."[569] China helped high American 2000s consumption by purchasing large quantities of U.S. Treasury bonds, which pay low interest rates and which America seriously needs China to keep buying.[570] Columnist and professor Martin Jacques called it a "Faustian bargain," saying that "the United States' position as the global financial centre and the dollar as the dominant reserve currency are on a Chinese life-support system."[571] Gabor Steingart called it a "diabolic pact,"[572] and Zakaria said it was "globalization's equivalent of the nuclear age's mutual assured destruction (MAD)."[573] In any case, China and the United States are so intractably dependent on each other that neither alone can viably change. The situation cannot easily be ended without doing great damage to both countries, and to many others. As Zachary Karabell said, the two economies have merged, and "they need us; we need them."[574] Zakaria also called it a "mutual suicide pact" and said the linkage would be best off slowly being removed.[575] Ferguson warned that if America and China stopped trading, globalization would end.[576]

With so much dependence on foreign trade, China is especially susceptible to protectionist measures elsewhere, which further American economic decline could cause.[577] If China sold United States Treasury bonds, or even stopped buying them, the value of their vast position therein would drop greatly.[578] As a saying goes, lend someone a dollar and you own them; lend someone a thousand dollars and they own you. As of 2008, China was the largest American creditor, buying mortgage-backed securities as well as the Treasury bonds;[579] the United States government's bailout of the mortgage-supporting Fannie Mae and Freddie Mac funds was, to a great extent, to protect Chinese interests.[580]

Might China change? Martin Jacques said that what he called the consensus view of China becoming internationally acquiescent was incorrect.[581] China views itself as a civilization instead of only a country, meaning that to Chinese their section of the world is, as Jacques put it, "akin to a geological formation in which the nation-state represents no more than the topsoil."[582] Chinese have historically seen their country as the Middle Kingdom, on a different level than other states and closer to heaven than are other parts of the world,[583] a status earned though the strength of its civilization.[584] Such Sinocentrism still undergirds Chinese patriotism.[585]

When the renminbi added 20% to its value from 2005 to 2008, Chinese imports on average only increased 2%.[586] Even if China were to allow its currency value to float, it could continue to cut costs to America and other customer countries. It is true that without the increase, Chinese prices might have fallen still lower, but there is real reason to question, after considering government intervention as well as market forces, whether a weak renminbi, artificially so or not, makes Chinese goods significantly cheaper than they would be otherwise.

For all its size and strength, China has a future which is, as Martin Ford put it, "highly unpredictable."[587] A 2007 Goldman Sachs study projected China in 2025 to be a close second in GDP to the United States and to have almost double America's GDP in 2050.[588] In 2008, the National Intelligence Council agreed that China would take over the top spot sometime after 2030.[589] However, the country also has many other concerns and vulnerabilities. For one thing, as was the case previously, China is heavily dependent on American export demand, which has already fallen with the 2008–2009 recession and may drop more. As of early 2009, the recession had already cost thousands of Chinese factories and millions of Chinese jobs.[590] As Martin Jacques said, if America and other countries experienced substantially shrinking economies with multi-year problems, China's growth rate would drop several percentage points, with possible civil disorder and its own continued unemployment problem, all of which would be even more devastating if, as before, Western countries became protectionist.[591] Second, China's low labor costs hold down domestic consumption but will not prevent further automation, so on both counts the country will be hard pressed to establish a huge middle class[592] and will not be fully developed for at least several more decades,[593] especially if its political system stays unchanged, as all developed nations except vastly-smaller Singapore are complete democracies.[594]

So how much longer can China's growth rate be sustained? Increased domestic consumer spending may be dependent on its people becoming more prosperous, which would require its workers to be paid more, which in turn would decrease its comparative advantage in low-cost manufacturing.[595] In 2005, Chinese economist Yu Yongding saw a 30% chance of large economic problems there.[596] Martin Jacques said that, regardless of the recession's outcome, "there are powerful reasons for believing that the present growth model is unsustainable in the long run, and probably even in the medium term" and that Chinese economic progress would undoubtedly tail off within 20 if not 10 years.[597] For its bad debts and huge export dependence, forecaster George Friedman called China "Japan on steroids" and said a simple dearth of skilled workers, or a necessary correction of the waste and inequities it has accumulated the past 30 years,[598] could stop its fast advance. Environmentalist Lester R. Brown determined that if the Chinese economy averaged 8% growth from 2006 through 2031, that year its per capita income would equal that of America 25 years before, which would call for it using 66% of the grain and twice the total amount of paper produced worldwide. If it also had 1.1 billion cars, those would be by themselves more than existed in 2006, and China would consume more oil than the world produced that year.[599]

Altogether, there is real doubt as to whether China will materialize as the world's main power. Martin Jacques claimed that neither slower economic growth nor fundamental Chinese political changes would derail it but acknowledged that "a twenty-first-century version of the intermittent bouts of introspection and instability" common to its history could.[600] George Friedman said China would not only fail to become a main 21st-century world power but would not likely even stay unified as a nation, as that would require Mao-style isolation.[601] Fareed Zakaria also questioned the Chinese government's ability to keep the country together going forward,[602] and Zachary Karabell noted that the United States is far from certain to be pushed out of its primary position.[603]

In any event, China's relationship with America is part of the world's political and economic landscape. Complaining about China or blaming it for United States problems is not only non-constructive and a distraction, but unjustified. Expecting to dominate a gigantic country with thousands of years of history would be beyond foolish. To a remarkably great extent, American prosperity has benefited from low Chinese prices at the cost, most likely, of jobs that could not have stayed in the United States anyway. We must look elsewhere for solutions to the problems posed by Work's New Age.

Upshot: Four Dead Ends

The areas here, more education and training, pursuing certain doubtful business activities, protectionist measures, and controlling or complaining about China, have two things in common. They are often mentioned as employment-crisis solutions, and they are not. So what might significantly help? The next three chapters address that.

Chapter 6:

Partial Solutions

*Without a doubt, this concept of "being your own boss"
is an alluring one. Not everyone can be a boss, however—at least not a good or successful one.*
—Eric Tyson and Jim Schell[604]

Cutting Immigration and Removing Foreign Workers: Will the L.A. Rastas Actually Take Lawn-Care Jobs?

The effect of immigrant workers on the employment crisis is the first I will explore of several polarizing possibilities. How can we assess it with even hands? Let us start with the facts.

The number of foreign-born people in America increased from 19.8 million in 1990 to 31.1 million in 2000[605] and reached 37 million in 2005.[606] As of that year 11.5 million were naturalized citizens, 14.4 million were in the country lawfully but not as citizens, and 11.1 million were in America illegally.[607] In 2006, about 21 million of those born elsewhere had jobs.[608] The portion of immigrants in the workforce was 5.2% in 1970 and has increased ever since, to 6.5% in 1980, 8.8% in 1990, about 13.3% in 2000, and 15.8% in 2007.[609]

Whether legal or illegal, newcomers usually have either very low or very high levels of education and job skills.[610] Many work in the United States for a short time, accept bad conditions, and then return home to buy a house, buy land, or launch a business.[611] In 2002, the average stay for an illegal resident was just over 16 months.[612] Employed immigrants tend to be between the ages of 20 and 40, prime working years when, as with Americans working overseas, their net return to employers may be the greatest.[613] As of 2006, non-native workers participated in the labor force at a higher rate than the general population, 69% to 66%, with undocumented Mexicans at 94%.[614]

Many illegal immigrants are paid under the table, but a large number use bogus Social Security numbers to work at jobs with formal payrolls and deductions. In that case, their wages are subject to the usual subtractions, from which they get no benefit.[615] Money for which the Social Security Administration does not have valid numbers is put in a suspense file, which may total as much as $7 billion per year.[616]

The percentage of native-born, working-age Americans without a high school degree dropped from 50% in 1960 to 12% in 2000.[617] Demand for employees needing little education is expected to rise more than for others,[618] yet constant-dollar pay for those not completing high school dropped from $13.45 to $11.38 per hour from 1973 to 2007, compared with a much smaller loss for high school graduates, a slight gain for those with some college, and substantial increases for college graduates and above.[619] In 2007, education levels of working immigrants averaged significantly lower than those born in America, with 29.1% of foreign-born employees having no high school diploma and lower percentages for all other levels, except for those with graduate degrees, where the share of immigrants was 11.1% compared with 9.9% of natives.[620] As of 2007, when almost one-third of foreign-born American workers were in California,[621] an estimated 40% of Los Angeles's population were immigrants, of whom three-fourths were there legally.[622]

Investigators have made a variety of findings. A 1997 National Research Council study determined that immigrants helped workers whom they complemented and hurt those who would otherwise substitute for them,[623] in effect concluding that newcomers generally do not compete with the majority of native-born Americans. In 2006, the country had 146 million workers, of whom about 7 million were unemployed and 21 million were foreign-born.[624] From 2000 to 2005, as the number of American-born men working dropped 1.7 million, 1.9 million new male immigrants joined the labor force.[625] In the year ending June 2010, native-born people lost a net total of 1.2 million jobs, while others gained 656,000.[626]

Although American workers without high school degrees have lower wages because of immigrant competition, which increases the supply of such labor,[627] and may have had their average pay drop doubled due to that,[628] the decline newcomers have caused has been only about 1% of their income.[629] Harvard economist George Borjas alternatively found that immigration from 1980 to 2000 caused a fall in earnings for all combinations of education level and sex.[630] One study of foreigners moving to California from 1960 to 2004 found no proof that it had degraded employment opportunities for American-born workers of similar skills and education,[631] and comparable research about the 1970s there discovered the same.[632] A 2003 Pew Hispanic Foundation study also concluded that there was no regular pattern showing any economic effect, positive or negative, on American-born workers from foreign-born ones.[633]

Population increases generate jobs as more people need more resources, many of which must be locally obtained,[634] one reason why removing non-native workers would be disadvantageous.[635] Additionally, as has been the case with agriculture in California, more expensive American workers may compel owners of labor-intensive companies to move to other countries.[636] Immigrants also often do jobs those born in America do not want;[637] as former Mexican president Vicente Fox controversially put it, newcomers work at "jobs that not even blacks want to do."[638] Many lower-skill immigrants also quickly lose their jobs during bad business times.[639] Yet even *Wall Street Journal* editor Jason L. Riley, author of the pro-immigration book *Let Them In*, wrote that if there was a labor shortage from a lack of newcomers, wages would adapt.[640] For example, in large parts of Europe, dry cleaning is considered an extravagance.[641] The question is whether we want such adaptation, since large labor cost increases in the food industry, to name one area, could cause big supermarket price hikes as well.[642]

What about the influx of highly-skilled and educated professionals such as doctors or scientists? In 1998, Cypress Semiconductors had 470 engineers. According to the CEO T.J. Rodgers, to support the products they designed, each needed about five other workers to manufacture, manage, and sell. Rodgers claimed that hiring the 172 foreign-born engineers created about 602 new jobs in America alone.[643] Mortimer P. Zuckerman opined that the number of H-1B visas for foreign graduate students, now receiving more than half of American masters' and doctoral degrees in the physical sciences, should be increased, as the alternative would be the students returning home after their education to "compete against us."[644] That view was shared by Microsoft chairman Bill Gates, who contended it would ultimately boost the number of American electronics manufacturing jobs.[645]

Pro- and anti-immigration writers each saw the opposite as worse for labor efficiency. Senior Federal Reserve Bank economist Pia Orrenius said a result of restricting immigration would be people doing jobs below their skill levels, "a fundamental misallocation of labor and a big inefficiency."[646] Center for Immigration Studies director Mark Krikorian, on the other hand, wrote that newcomers' wage-lowering effect cuts motivation to use labor more effectively and slows innovation, including robotics, and he equated Japanese use of robots with Americans employing Mexicans.[647]

What might happen if more foreigners of all education and skill levels were allowed to work in the United States? Wider-range immigration, if new arrivals were paid less, could result in sharply lower wages for large sections of existing Americans.[648] Another result could be a large decrease in the number of United States citizens completing degrees, be they high school, college, or graduate, with Mark Krikorian mentioning the possibility that attending college would become "a job Americans won't do."[649]

It is not reasonable to attribute all job losses by native-born people to newcomers. However, with jobs paying middling wages bearing the brunt of cuts since 1990,[650] massive immigration of moderately- educated and skilled workers, as opposed to those in the top few percent for whom allowing entry seems clearly desirable, could greatly worsen the labor surplus. On the other side, those on the lower end do not seem to present the same problem. Would uneducated, American-born people take the low-end jobs illegal and other immigrants have been doing? If so, why are so many still unemployed? If the choice is then between robots or Mexicans, it is hardly clear that Mexicans are worse—the $7 billion unused-benefit subsidy, as well as additional jobs needed to provide them goods and services, make a strong case for less skilled foreign workers. So for Work's New Age, hold off the middle where it's crowded, but let the ends in.

Startups and Other Entrepreneurial Activity— Not All the Same, Not for All, and Not All Work

Many times recently, new businesses or startups have been credited with contributing many American jobs. Fed chairman Ben Bernanke said in July 2010 that small businesses begun in the prior two years had, during the previous 20 years, employed 10% of all people working but created 25% of all new positions. Senior research fellow Tim Kane held that companies in their first 12 months start about three million jobs a year, while all other firms together end more than they create.[651]

There are three things we should understand about this data. First, it is important to realize that small businesses in general, also often credited with generating jobs, are not the same as new businesses and that once the new companies are factored out, there is no relationship between job creation and company size.[652] Second, startups perforce create jobs, since before they existed they had none. Third, not all new businesses have the same employment significance. Some entrepreneurs leave their positions and work hundred-hour weeks, some are independently wealthy and go into business more for fun than for income, and some keep their office jobs and sell Mary Kay products on the side. Some are sole proprietorships with no employees, and some are 20-person incorporated ventures. In effect, new ventures may add zero, one, or many new jobs, yet all turn up in the numbers.

Working at a serious small business is a challenge at which not many people, especially those who have specialized in a limited number of areas before,[653] can succeed. Such efforts typically call for many roles, such as dealing with problematic customers,[654] sales, buying, accounting, marketing, management, and janitorial work,[655] along with hiring, firing, training and motivating workers, payroll, budgeting, and working with lawyers and bankers.[656] Small-company owners must be strongly self-motivated, and hours are usually long.[657] In their introductory volume *Small Business for Dummies*, authors Eric Tyson and Jim Schell present a suitability quiz for running one's own venture. It indicates the valued qualities are business interest, perseverance under adversity, high energy, ability to research and implement difficult decisions, optimism, preference for activity over idleness, related work experience, creativity, rebounding from failure, natural leadership, and discipline—a list on which many if not most would score low. They also mention confidence, intuition, drive, and passion[658] but make it clear that if a business has no reasonable chance of becoming profitable, it should be discontinued without regard for the owner's pride.[659]

Eric Tyson and Jim Schell name advantages of owning a company, such as personal satisfaction, independence, more control over scheduling, and monetary potential.[660] However, the drawbacks are also considerable and include great responsibility, dealing with competition and much change, coping with many random factors, complying with government requirements, and the chance of losing one's entire (and possibly large) investment in a failure.[661] Potential proprietors are strongly urged to settle all personal consumer debt before starting and then reduce their own expenses as low as reasonably possible.[662] Business owners must also obtain their own benefits, which can cost a lot without a job providing them.[663]

Because of these factors, among others, not many Americans are self-employed full time. Although Robert J. Samuelson wrote in 2010 that "the entrepreneurial instinct seems deeply ingrained in the nation's economic culture,"[664] and many others before him have agreed, some data supports a different view. According to a 2007 study, only 7.2% of Americans are self-employed, trailing Canada, Australia, New Zealand, and 16 countries in Western Europe, ahead of only Luxembourg. Most differences were significant, with the bulk of the developed countries listed between 10.6% and 14.4%, and some were huge—Ireland, New Zealand, Spain, Portugal, and Italy had 16.8% to 26.4%, while Greece reported 35.9% self-employed, almost five times America's rate.[665]

Over all, new businesses are valuable. But in terms of maintaining jobs, we may need to adapt the adage that it is cheaper to keep existing customers than to get new ones. Repeat customers can last for years, even decades, if conditions are favorable for them, and the same is true for employment. If the vast majority of 2010 startups' jobs will be gone by 2015, then we have to wonder if such an emphasis on new companies is truly justified.

Small business participation is no broad-based answer. Despite the independence in American national character, most by far want to work for others. About half of all new businesses fail.[666] In the 2008–2009 recession, small company sales severely declined,[667] and economist and former Harvard president Larry Summers called the spring 2010 situation "a quiet depression in small business."[668] As for entrepreneurial efforts being jobs, many are not. We must consider the frequent lack of gainful income before seeing business ventures as employment, and that should cause us to factor down their numbers. Hardly any people working for others do not take in more than they spend for their labors, but if ten million people go into business and only half of them show a net profit, then the effect on employment is the same as if only five million of them were working and the other five million spent time and money on other projects. So I give partial credit, no less but no more, to entrepreneurism as a solution to Work's New Age.

Sales Jobs: No Hard Way Out Anymore

Sales work has long been known as an area where people could get a chance when others were difficult to find. The idea was simple: You tried to sell something, you were paid only or almost only if you made sales, and if you didn't succeed, you would lose your job. Employers would be much more willing to take you on, since either you would make money for them or you would be gone. So how are sales jobs doing now?

In the 1950s, 1960s, and 1970s, sales positions increased in number more than most other livelihoods. In the 1980s, they grew more than those in any other employment category, but the progression stopped soon thereafter, and there was a net loss in 2007.[669] In recessions past, sales jobs did not suffer as much. With the advantage to employers mentioned above, why can't sales positions help large numbers of the unemployed? There are four main reasons.

> **WORK'S NEW AGE PRINCIPLE #11**
>
> **If ten million people go into business and half lose money, then only five million had the equivalent of jobs.**

First, since 2008, even those with much sales success behind them have been losing jobs and not finding new ones.[670] Second, the Internet has made many sales positions unnecessary,[671] which in effect is simply another example of automation replacing workers. Third, most sales jobs constitute self-employment,[672] thus, as before, are not suitable for most Americans. Fourth, the qualities they require are different from other positions. Many in the field are hung up on, have doors closed on them, and are avoided socially[673]—they need to overcome the profession's stigma, including decades of negative media depictions.[674] Those successful in sales consider almost any time possible for finding prospects,[675] and beyond that they need a high overall level of personal commitment, more than for most jobs, to succeed,[676] so many leave for lack of it.[677] In all, though many people excel at sales and some will always be required, the number of people compatible with, seeking, and now needed for sales positions is too small to constitute more than a very minor improvement to Work's New Age.

Economic Stimulus Money—The Great Argument-Starter

Problems with the economy in 2008 and 2009 did not respond to the usual solutions of cutting interest rates and increasing government spending.[678] A $787 billion federal government economic stimulus package designed to preserve and generate jobs and thereby raise overall demand for goods and services[679] was approved in 2009.[680] As a result, the economy improved from what Robert J. Samuelson called "virtual free fall" to relative stability.[681]

Around the beginning of 2010, three research concerns, HIS Global Insight, Macroeconomic Advisers, and Moody's Economy.com, projected a savings from the stimulus, the American Recovery and Reinvestment Act,[682] of 2.5 million jobs.[683] In July 2010, journalist John Harwood, writing for *The New York Times*, said 2.5 million,[684] and the White House Council of Economic Advisers put the range at 2.5 million to 3.6 million.[685] The Congressional Budget Office judged in an August 2010 report that somewhere from 1.4 million to 3.3 million more people were working that month than would have been if the act had not passed. Economists Alan Blinder and Mark Zandi estimated 2.7 million saved.[686] As of October 2010, the Congressional Budget Office assessed that the stimulus reduced unemployment from 11.6% to the then-current rate of 9.6%.[687]

Larry Summers compared the September 2008 crash with the Cuban missile crisis, saying that we might never know how close the U.S. economic and financial structures were to a complete breakdown.[688] Indeed, as the crash actually happened, from their

2006 and 2007 overall peaks through October 2010, nationwide home equity had dropped a total of $6.5 trillion, stock portfolios fell $4.3 trillion, and further unassessed losses came from 7.7 million jobs gone.[689] In one quarter, household net worth plunged $5 trillion, or 30%, an all-time record.[690] The recovery was so quick after the first bailout that as of September 2010, the government was expected to recover almost 90% of the money. Fareed Zakaria maintained that "the American system had a heart attack and we responded fast and well."[691]

Not all about stimuli are positive. Quantitative easing, a synonym for printing more money, is dangerous when used simply for stimulus. Another effort to spur demand through quantitative easing, in the trillions, might cause a large drop in the dollar's value.[692]

It may be too difficult or too politically charged to accurately determine the true cost or merit of stimuli, but the 2009 one seems to have at the least headed off chaos, catastrophic damage to confidence, and possibly even civil disorder. Stimuli are extreme emergency measures, and their use for purposes other than appropriately grave crises may be severely destructive. Such are the decisions forced upon us by the realities of Work's New Age.

Upshot: Better, But Not Enough

These four possibilities all have value. New business efforts, sales jobs, and limiting middle-level immigration could together benefit many people, and government stimuli, if justified and while dangerous, could help almost everyone. In addition, foreign employment, if it can be counted as a valid solution, could be useful for some also. In the next chapter, I will move on to even better ideas.

Chapter 7:

Valuable Possibilities

Health insurance is not something that is made better by tying it to employment. As a result, essentially all economists believe that universal coverage should be done outside of employment. —David M. Cutler[693]

Back to the WPA

In September 2010, President Obama's staff broached the possibility of a $50 billion public works employment bill.[694] That plan was not broad-based though, as it was simply for surface transportation[695] and represented only a small fraction of the $1.2 trillion the American Society of Civil Engineers said that year that maintaining American highways and bridges, to name just one possible construction area, would cost.[696]

There are a variety of points in favor of American infrastructure work being done soon. First, it could be a relatively quick way of getting people jobs.[697] Robert Scott suggests that heavy spending on infrastructure would help American business's international competitiveness, a view shared by Bob Herbert.[698] In mid-2010, construction costs dropped to a multi-year low with labor, helped by 17% unemployment in the field and commercial loans not only available but at discounted rates not seen previously.[699] Affordable housing units would be valuable in much greater numbers than exist today.

As well as building, environmental cleanups and maintenance would be a worthy area for WPA-style programs.[700] William Julius Wilson made a case in 1996 for public works jobs to help inner-city residents, in large part a recommendation to help lower their high unemployment rate.[701] Jeremy Rifkin in 1995 quoted an investment analyst saying that such a program, while costing $250 billion in contemporary dollars, could create as many as a million jobs for each of ten years.[702] Columnist Ezra Klein wrote that if the government were acting as a business on the lookout for winning opportunities, it would have one here.[703]

One case against programs in which the government directly hires is that they may cost private companies business and workers. They may also seem socialistic to some, and may be hard to push through legislatively.[704] Yet the twin advantages of providing jobs and completing infrastructure work almost certain to be needed anyway make extra public works employment a clear winner.

Separate Health Care from Jobs

A second form of job lock, after people's limits on moving to other areas, has been their health care coverage. The connection of health insurance to work was never an intended national policy as such.[705] Although 60% of Americans under 65 have health coverage through employers, and most of them are satisfied with it,[706] many companies still do not provide it. One effect of that is people choosing to work for those with health plans rather going where their services would otherwise be most valuable.[707]

The low self-employment rate seems to connect with health insurance. Often when coverage is purchased separately, its price is very high,[708] and if jobs provide it, not only is that crucial need assured of being met but the employer-paid premiums are not taxed. Indeed, 2009 research implied that losing job-connected health coverage discouraged many from leaving work to start businesses,[709] so much American self-employment is only part time. Entrepreneurial professor Scott Shane concluded that "the health care mess is clearly weighing down entrepreneurship in this country."[710]

As well as costing more and more for workers, employer-based health insurance is burdensome on companies in various ways. One is the effect it has on pricing, and, in competing for exports, the difference can be large.[711] Former Chrysler chairman Lee Iacocca once said American automakers spent more money per car on health insurance than they did on steel.[712] That may now be an understatement, as in 2004 General Motors spent $5 billion, or about $1,400 per vehicle, on health care.[713] Employees themselves continue to pay for those increasing costs through forgoing what would probably otherwise be higher cash compensation.[714] As a result, many companies, especially small ones,[715] will seek information on potential employees' health problems and, legally or not, base hiring decisions on it.[716] If part-time workers have no health benefits, more jobs will be of that type as insurance costs increase.[717] In one way or another—either through losing profitability, raising prices, or releasing workers—businesses, employees, customers, and others connected with them are hurt when health insurance costs rise.[718]

How much will the 2010 law help in disconnecting work from health care? The exchanges will guarantee coverage is available, not only for those with no employer or otherwise guaranteed insurance but also for those with expensive or incomplete coverage from work.[719] Companies will still have primary health care responsibility, though,

> ### WORK'S NEW AGE PRINCIPLE #12
>
> **Although America has no universal health care, its government all by itself paid more per person than those of eight other developed countries with coverage for all.**

and rising costs therefore may be slowed but will not go away.

Is the American health arrangement—with so many different programs, it isn't really a system—too good to be replaced? That is another area of great disagreement, with most in one camp or the other, but some facts must be considered. As of 2010, the United States had the 49th highest life expectancy and 49th lowest infant death rate.[720] That year, of the 19 countries with highest per capita income, America ranked last in "avoidable mortality," including asthma, diabetes, and kidney disease.[721] As of 2010, 51 million United States citizens were uninsured, many of whom contributed to shortcomings in health outcomes by getting care too late or not at all.[722] And although, as above, most with employer-based plans were happy with them, in 1999 only 20% of Americans thought the entire health care structure performed effectively.[723] European nations, with universal health care usually unattached to employers, are now spending about 8% of their GDPs on it, far below the American proportion.[724] Some 1998 percentages of GDP spent on health care were 6.7% for the United Kingdom, 7.6% for Japan, 9.5% for Canada, 10.6% for Germany, and 13.6% for the United States.[725] As of 2005, America led a group of 20 developed countries with health care costs at 15.3% of GDP, with next highest being Switzerland at 11.6% and the 18 others in a range from 11.1% (France) down to 7.5% (Ireland and Finland). Although a greater part of American expenses were paid privately than any of the other 19, U.S. *governmentally paid* health care costs had higher GDP percentages than those of Greece, Australia, Netherlands, Italy, Spain, Japan, Ireland, or Finland, all of which had vastly lower privately-covered shares.[726]

One problem with leaving health care to the free market is that with health issues the relationship between supply and demand is distorted. As those who provide the care have much more knowledge and information than patients about what products or services are desirable, and to what extents, doctors and others respond comparatively little to what customers say they want and instead select or at least influence what is chosen.[727] As for the connection with work, all Canadians and Britons have health care unaffected by their employment or lack of it,[728] and their countries since 1970 have had lower increases in proportion to GDP than Germany, Japan, or America,[729] for which that is not the case.[730] One reason European workers put in fewer hours may be that American employers, who pay health care costs per worker, have an interest in minimizing the number of employees by increasing the time each works.[731]

Many do not realize there are already several total-entrée health care systems in the United States. The largest is Medicare, which from 1999 to 2009 had slower cost increases than those of private insurance plans. Public support for a comprehensive, single-payer American health care system was about 50% in 2009.[732] And how different is American health care from that in other countries anyway? The combination of payment methods may be unique, but the systems within it are not. As *Washington Post* global correspondent T.R. Reid described, Americans with jobs have private insurance plans with partial patient payments like Germans, senior citizens are treated like Canadians with copays and set fees, Indians and veterans have fully-government-paid coverage like those in Great Britain, and the uninsured are, as concerns health care, living in a third-world country.[733]

On the other hand, two thoughts are worthy of consideration. First, the split in health outcomes between United States residents insured and uninsured is probably great, a gap which cannot be charged to health plans. Second, American choices for freedom may mean more people opt for risky lifestyles, which worsen health results in their own right. Yet the overwhelming preponderance of evidence calls for a major change, beyond the 2010 law, in how American health care is provided. We can debate how well the free market works for health care, but not sensibly on its attachment to work; over all, as Martin Ford contended, with so many jobs disappearing, it is unworkable for health coverage to be tied to employment.[734] I see disconnecting this link one of the best things we can do for Work's New Age.

More Unemployment Benefits

Timothy M. Sneeding of the University of Wisconsin said the country had "a work-based safety net without any work."[735] While unemployment payments make it less attractive for people to take jobs,[736] and according to one late-2009 study doing without that year's extension would have reduced unemployment from

10.0% to 9.6%,[737] extending jobless payments helps those without work, particularly the long-term unemployed, stay afloat.[738] Also, putting money in the hands of those especially likely to spend it on goods and services fuels the economy at relatively low expense and risk, to the point where Moody's economist Mark Zandi said unemployment insurance was among the best stimulus methods.[739]

I think the last point carries the issue. As we have seen, and with five officially unemployed people alone for each February 2011 job opportunity,[740] we're way past the point where all of those working and able to work can do so. Therefore benefits should be lengthened, at least consistently with today's longer unemployment times.

Living without So Much Work

How about choosing a lifestyle that doesn't require a full-time job? That is possible, and millions of Americans have been living that way for decades. Here I will describe two general possibilities involving very low spending, one rural and one town or urban.

The countryside version, as it is now commonly lived, often includes a lack of links to municipal infrastructure. As of 2007, there were about 300,000 American households without connection to government-provided electricity, water, and heat, a number that had been expected to grow to 520,000 homes with close to one million people by 2010.[741] Many of its newest participants lost jobs during the 2008–2009 recession or perceived all other options were worse.[742] Those who lived this way before were generally from both ends of the political spectrum, either liberal anti-capitalists or conservative survivalists and rural Southerners.[743]

Characteristics of a back-to-the-land lifestyle can include growing food; heating with paper, cardboard, and wood from trees and abandoned buildings in often homemade stoves; bartering; buying clothing used; and generally obtaining as many living solutions as possible from the environment.[744] Some actively want to reduce their need to pay money for things and resist seeing wealth as a form of status.[745] Those raising children often homeschool them and value living in a community where there is little peer pressure to buy them expensive toys.[746] Common religious choices include Anabaptist (Amish or Mennonite), other Christian, Zen Buddhist, pagan, and atheist.[747] While some consider living off the land a political deed,[748] others are unconcerned that way. Some draw inspiration from the 5th century B.C. Athenian Diogenes, who at one point lived purposefully without any possessions.[749] They usually own their homes, which may be trailers,[750] abandoned,[751] or otherwise not mainstream houses. With the help of used construction materials and self-manufacture, they usually owe no money on them,[752] which some say is a critical component to the lifestyle.[753] Some work occasionally and some permanently but part time,[754] while others earn money through such means as babysitting, doing housework for others, breeding and selling animals, and selling plants, all on a small scale.[755] They often do not have cars and usually walk or bicycle for transportation.[756] Work at home and on the land generally takes them several hours a day, varying greatly by season.[757]

People choosing to live in the country with low expenses often do so to be freed of mortgages, mass marketing, and being tied to a working life. They want to live more independently and environmentally soundly, though many are greener only unintentionally.[758] Modern electronic connections can be managed though wireless modems and car battery power.[759] Expenses have potential to be extremely low—one interviewee claimed that with a home owned outright and growing his own food, he could live for $150 per month.[760] Some with this lifestyle generally think it is harder to pay for many things than it is to do without them.[761] As clear disadvantages, though, they usually have no insurance[762] and minimal health care.[763]

On the more urban alternative, two authors, Bob Clyatt[764] and Jacob Lund Fisker,[765] have written about life in semiretirement, which Clyatt describes as the process of using all means at one's disposal to live independently without working full time.[766]

Many considerations are similar to those of the rural people above, including avoiding many ways to spend money.[767]

Several things that people with town or city low-expense lifestyles do to manage expenses include cutting their own hair, repairing clothing, cooking from fresh ingredients, buying used in general, choosing public or self-powered transportation, using libraries, growing vegetables, making some household products usually bought, and self-maintaining their cars, motorcycles, and bicycles.[768] Exchanging unneeded items through organized or community systems for those personally useful, along with reusing,[769] conserves money also. As with the frugal rural residents, some consider that children do not need as many high-priced toys and electronic devices as others might think, and discussing the family's financial situation and budget truthfully with them may help, along with reinforcing that less money means less time away for work and therefore more with them.[770] To reduce housing costs, they live in smaller quarters or share them with others, limit insurance to that which covers true financial disasters,[771] buy older cars, eat ordinary food, and avoid wasting heat or electricity.[772]

A low-expense mindset can be understood by considering the spending habits of many who lived through the Great Depression.[773] Another way is budgeting amounts for each large category and recording all money spent.[774] In general, efficiency and decreasing waste are important,[775] and many couples with frugal city and town lifestyles are able to live on less than $25,000 per year.[776]

A third possibility is to move to a country where retirees or semi-retirees can live cheaply but decently. Some possibilities are Costa Rica, the Dominican Republic, Ecuador, Mexico, Panama, Thailand, and Vietnam.[777] Less unusual places for many might be rural Portugal, rural France, or New Zealand, where semi-retired people could fit in with others living simply.[778]

When less of it is needed for one's lifestyle, work can fall into several categories. Those which Bob Clyatt named included "the filler job," or a reasonably pleasant but low-paying steady position;

"the avocation," or a job one might take on even if it were unpaid; "your former job, but less of it," maybe without benefits; and "hobby turned business," if profitable.[779] Those living frugally also consider it important to discover other meaningful activity.[780] One danger the authors see for hard-driving people starting low-expense lifestyles is to be too intense about work, which can be offset by consciously calming down, delaying key decisions until a year after ending the full-time job, or just accepting it.[781]

A frugal lifestyle, whether on or off the power and communications grids, has clear disadvantages—it can be very austere in ways which Americans are used to more comfort, for one thing—but the ideas behind it offer something to almost everyone. Now that we are in a time of lower general affluence, it behooves us to evaluate what is essential. For most of us, if we neither need something nor greatly want it, we should consider doing without it. Assessing what is truly valuable to us is a critical skill for Work's New Age.

Cheaper Food by Putting Farm Subsidies Out to Pasture

Farm product subsidies and tariffs date from the 1930s, when in 1933 President Franklin D. Roosevelt approved the Agricultural Adjustment Act. Farm incomes had then dropped two-thirds in three years,[782] and the measures were meant to help safeguard small farmers.[783] They continued after World War II for protection from price and weather uncertainty.[784] From the 1960s through the 1980s, many family farms were consolidated into corporate structures[785] without any reduction in governmental aid. All told, there were 15 legal acts authorizing farm subsidies between 1933 and 2002. Together, they were known as "omnibus legislation," which means they included a wide variety of laws and authorizations, in these cases regarding food stamps, forestry, and food safety.[786]

Those receiving subsidies are authorized by crop, not by size or need—as a farmer or corporation plants more, they increase.[787] From 1995 to 2004, 80% of commodity subsidies were for corn, cotton, wheat, rice, and soybeans.[788] Subsidies tend to be higher when farm prices are lower, as in 2005, when the $20 billion paid out was relatively high.[789]

From 1970 to 2007, the American government funded a total of $578 billion in farm subsidies.[790] In 2002, $4 billion went to cotton alone,[791] and in 2006 the same amount supported corn.[792] As of 2010, government spent $10 billion to $30 billion each year subsidizing farmers, mostly very large ones, with $5 billion in payments without regard to crop production, $4 billion to purchase crop insurance, and as much as $4 billion for bad-year protection.[793] Around 2009, farm subsidies cost the average taxpayer $322 per year.[794]

While the payments have continued for 80 years, the nature of farming in the United States has changed greatly. From 1932, around the time of the first subsidies, to 2002, the number of American farms dropped from 6.7 million to 2.1 million,[795] with mean size climbing from 213 acres in 1950 to 434 in 2000.[796] Per capita farm income, in 1934 one-third of the American average, was in 2004 26% above it, and at the same time the share of those living on farms fell from 25% to 2%.[797] As of 2005, America had only 2 million farmers and just 350,000 of them worked at it full time,[798] and the largest 150,000 American farms produced more than half of the country's total output of food and fiber.[799]

So who is getting the money? As the Heritage Foundation wrote, most subsidies now go to "large farms, agribusinesses, politicians and celebrity hobby farmers." Subsidies, far removed from their origins of protecting poor farmers, have become the country's chief benefit scheme for corporations,[800] with Manulife Financial, MeadWestvaco, Chevron Texaco, and Caterpillar among those receiving at least $320,000 in 2002.[801] Between 1995 and 2005, 10% of subsidy recipients received 75% of the payments, averaging $91,000 per year.[802] In 2002, two companies in Stuttgart, Arkansas, Riceland Foods and Producers Rice Mill, received $110 million and $83.9 million, respectively. Some people collecting more than $100,000 in farm subsidies from

1995 to 2002 included Representative Cal Dooley, Rep. Doug Ose, Rep. Tom Latham, Senator Mike DeWine, Sen. Charles Grassley, television network owner Ted Turner, and basketball player Scottie Pippen.[803]

The broad nature of the Farm Bills and that they are commonly referred to under that name has the effect of putting them in a category with which most people are not directly involved, meaning that few people are aware of their contents.[804] One, the Farm Security and Rural Investment Act of 2002, which might have been the most extravagant of all time, attracted comments such as "shockingly awful" from *The Washington Post* and "a 10-year, $173.5 billion bucket of slop" from *The Wall Street Journal*.[805] The cost of such programs to consumers is considerable; as one example, economist Daniel Sumner estimated that if subsidies and the governmental pricing system were removed, a gallon of milk sold retail in Chicago would be about 20 cents cheaper.[806] If tariffs alone, which cost American consumers money by stopping them from buying less expensive imported food, were discontinued, Americans would save $2 billion.[807]

When asked if there was a good case to be made for farm subsidies, Daniel Sumner's response was "no," claiming their only justification was traditional.[808] Robert J. Samuelson called agriculture "the economy's most pampered, protected and subsidized sector," when asked, in the event of no subsidies, if "Iowa's cornfields and Kansas's wheat fields [would] go fallow", and he said the subsidies hurt national interests by impeding trade negotiations.[809] Author Daniel Imhoff wrote that subsidies had become "a corporate boondoggle,"[810] and *Wall Street Journal* correspondents Roger Thurow and Scott Kilman called them "a matter of addiction."[811]

In all, farm subsidies are high on the list of government programs that have outlived their justifications and are now simply costly and destructive. Their problems include, but are not limited to, those of the protectionism that they are (especially higher prices at the grocery store), and that they benefit few of generally doubtful need at the expense of many. In addition to their employment and financial harm, their connection with the nation's obesity problem has been well documented.[812] The title of a *Newsweek* editorial urging cutting of subsidies, "Here's an Easy One,"[813] could not be more appropriate.

Lower Consumer Prices: A Good Thing

Wal-Mart, all by itself, has done a great deal to lift American prosperity. Its offerings may not appear as changes in the Consumer Price Index, but in many cases they have transformed small purchases into trivial ones, significant purchases into small ones, and unusual luxuries into goods priced for many to afford. As one example, in the 2000s, DVD players usually cost $200 to $400, but once Wal-Mart negotiated better pricing from Chinese suppliers, they sold for $100 and became vastly more common.[814] As low prices are good for unemployed people as well as others, and, as mentioned above, manufacturing in America may not be viable anyway, we should encourage them without qualification.

Tax Cuts in the Right Places

Tax improvements for businesses, such as the 1977–78 New Jobs Tax Credit,[815] can spur them to hire more workers.[816] One set of research concluded in 2010 that such a benefit could increase jobs by 250,000 to 727,000, depending on incentive sizes.[817] In his 2010 State of the Union address, President Obama asked for federal tax credits for companies generating American jobs, along with increasing taxes on those hiring in other countries,[818] but he also asked to raise them on singles earning at least $200,000 per year and families with annual net incomes of $250,000 or more, which would impede spending by a group comprising almost 25% of consumer outlay.[819] William P. Quigley of Loyola University New Orleans recommended not only tax breaks for adding workers but for keeping them.[820] Others agreeing with tax incentives for hiring included Timothy Bartik of the W.E. Upjohn Institute, writer Charles Cerami, and Robert Haveman of the University of Wisconsin.[821] Martin Ford advocated replacing payroll levies entirely with a gross margin tax, which would be affected less by job losses.[822]

On the other side, as tax credits for adding employees can easily be manipulated, they have often done poorly.[823] Employers may not choose to hire anyway; skipping, say, $5,000 in payroll taxes for each new worker would save only 10% of an average first year's compensation.[824] However, there is too much potential in this area to abandon it. Even if companies save taxes by hiring workers they would have added anyway, they are still hiring, and any outright fraud can be dealt with directly. Improving the tax structure to account for jobs created, and maybe even saved, should be public policy in Work's New Age.

Down with the Minimum Wage

The first federal minimum wage, 25 cents per hour, took effect in 1938.[825] As Figure 25 shows, since 1973 its constant dollar value has generally declined, but it has been within a moderate range, between $5.50 and $8 in 2009 money.[826]

There has been controversy about the effect of the minimum wage on jobs. Per William P. Quigley as of 2003, none of the 18 times it had increased caused a higher unemployment rate,[827] though Jared Bernstein and Jeff Chapman of the Economic Policy Institute concluded that at times minimum wage raises had caused small drops in the number working.[828]

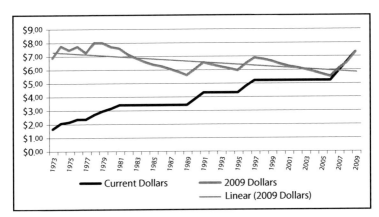

Figure 25: Minimum Wage in Current and Constant Dollars, 1973–2009 – 1947–1972 average: $6.45

One point in favor of a lower minimum wage is that it serves the free market. In the most expensive areas, that rate is practically unknown, as labor there is worth more. The minimum wage applies only in places where prices are lower, so reducing it will affect only jobs where the value of work is less. Although people cannot support others or possibly even themselves on what a minimum-wage position pays, not all need to, and putting such a burden on jobs is unrealistic, especially when there is not enough work anyway. Additionally, a reduction could allow people to hire workers for tasks not worth the current minimum wage to them. Ultimately, I believe a lower minimum, which would hardly have a universal effect on workers, would both create jobs and reduce prices, both valuable outcomes for Work's New Age.

Fewer Hours per Worker, Finally?

Before the 1700s, work took up most of people's waking time. The first Industrial Revolution workweek was 70 hours, which for most was actually an improvement.[829] As productivity increased, that time dropped.[830] American labor unions pushed for the 40-hour week in the late 1860s, motivated by, among other things, decreasing unemployment.[831] That same rationale influenced the federal government as well when it required 40-hour weeks[832] and sanctioned them in the Wage and Hour Act of 1938.[833]

Many observers over the years have thought the future would bring shorter working hours.[834] Around 1970, futurist Alvin Toffler forecast that, as a result of automation and technology, the 21st century would bring more leisure and less time on the job.[835] In 1979, computer scientist Christopher Evans projected that by 2000, workdays would drop to five or even four hours.[836] As of 1988, some still expected workweeks to drop to at most 28 hours.[837] Yet the reality was better exemplified by General Motors autoworkers in 1994 demanding an end to mandatory overtime, or in fact only reinstating the 40-hour week in place of a de facto longer one.[838]

So how could we achieve less time on the job? Jeremy Rifkin proposed in 2004 that a shorter workweek corresponding to productivity gains should be officially sanctioned for all, with the government paying the difference between 35 hours and 39 or 40 in cash or reduced taxes.[839] In 2009, Martin Ford saw government-subsidized job sharing as an improvement over laying off some people and allowing others to be supported without working.[840] Betsey Stevenson, not in favor of a mandated shorter workweek, nevertheless said in 2010 that while a majority would prefer all workers having their hours cut 20% to one-fifth of them being laid off, most states' unemployment insurance would then pay nothing.[841] If the missing day were covered, the arrangement could be called "unemployment insurance-supported work sharing,"[842] which was used in Germany[843] and Canada as well as in some American states.[844]

A similar option, job sharing, or reduced hours for reduced pay, is instead a permanent choice for workers at some companies[845] and does not involve unemployment compensation. Possibilities for decreasing workers' hours without shortening the official workweek include sabbaticals, early retirement, and individual voluntary cuts, along with various opportunities to attend school instead of work.[846] One advantage of job sharing in place of layoffs is keeping more people, with differing skills, on staff.[847] With it, many Australian employees reported higher productivity, especially as the arrangement limited their hours, and companies there reported lower turnover and more happiness[848] among its participants. Job-sharing firms could also more easily resume full hours in place of firing and then hiring, if workloads justified that.[849]

All in all, it was once considered a boon to be able to work less. More than 140 years ago, a slogan for what is still the most commonly thought-of workday length was "eight hours labor, eight hours rest and eight hours for what we will."[850] Someday we may look back at 40-plus-hour weeks as barbaric. In Work's New Age, if health care can be disconnected from work, we have an opportunity to rediscover the value of less time on the job.

Upshot: The Best We Have, Unless...

The ideas presented in this chapter are the best I have seen. The federal government can help by lowering the minimum wage, starting a new WPA-type program, ending farm subsidies, cutting taxes in ways that boost employment, and favoring low product prices in general. Federal or state governments can assist by lengthening and perhaps raising unemployment benefits. Businesses can contribute by shortening workweeks instead of discharging workers. People having trouble finding the employment they want can help themselves by living in ways that do not need as much income. The best thing I can do in this chapter, though, is to cut the chain between health care and jobs, which is the key to the success of many ideas above and elsewhere.

If implemented, these possibilities would greatly mitigate the problems of Work's New Age. But for how long would they be enough for us to weather an ever-shrinking number of jobs? There is one more option we must seriously consider, and I will look at it in the next chapter.

Chapter 8:

Thinking the Not-So-Unthinkable: Guaranteed Income

The key point about guaranteed income, quite correctly perceived, is that it means we will no longer allow people to starve nor to become increasingly enslaved by and to work. —Stanley Aronowitz, Dawn Esposito, William DiFazio, and Margaret Yard[851]

If joblessness continues to rise, Americans could face a vast increase in the need for unemployment payments and other government services at a time of falling tax revenues.[852] To solve that matter permanently, various observers have proposed comprehensive systems of government-provided compensation. I will consider five different options along that line.

The Possibilities

One idea, which Jeremy Rifkin called a "shadow wage," would not be a direct payment but a tax benefit providing a certain amount for each volunteer hour worked. It is a similar concept to tax deductions for charitable contributions.[853] These credits could be the same for time given to any registered charitable organization or, in the case of agreed-upon variation in need for volunteers, made higher for the most pressing causes.[854]

One step beyond the shadow wage would be to pay people for working in an expanded set of government-provided nonprofit jobs, an idea circulating in American economic circles since at least 1963, when economists Robert Theobald and Robert Heilbroner, among others, advocated it.[855] This thought, which Jeremy Rifkin labeled "a social wage," would involve providing money for those who seem permanently unemployed to be trained for and work at positions in nonprofit organizations.[856] Pay would vary with the qualifications of the worker and the job involved.[857] The social wage idea has in effect been successfully practiced over the past several decades, under the names of Volunteers in Service to America (VISTA), the Peace Corps, AmeriCorps,[858] and workfare.[859] Many commentators who would not consent to "rights without responsibilities" have accepted the idea of a social wage,[860] as it offers payment for work instead of, in the case of unemployment benefits, payment for trying to work,[861] which then goes away when the recipient becomes economically productive.[862]

Beyond the social wage is what Martin Ford called "virtual jobs."[863] These would not require work as such but would pay differing amounts for activity in pursuits deemed salutary, such as education, environmental stewardship, and conceivably but controversially personal health, as well as for municipal and local activities.[864] Ford suggests that incentives could be set by a governmental or semi-private organization.[865]

Another possibility is William P. Quigley's idea of a constitutional amendment guaranteeing all Americans jobs.[866] He perceived great public support for that idea, which could involve public or private positions, all with a minimum rate of pay based on presence or lack of health insurance and the worker's family size.[867] Quigley claimed as his precursors Thomas Paine and President Franklin D. Roosevelt[868] and considered the wage floor especially important, since in the 1990s, more than 75% of American families in poverty had at least one member working part-time or more.[869] Quigley saw no lack of useful work that could be performed, and in addition to WPA-style construction projects, child care or providing recreational activities would be valuable.

A bolder idea than the social wage would be to pay people directly with no clear requirements. This notion goes back to the 18th century, to Thomas Paine, Henri de Saint-Simon, and, later, Bertrand Russell.[870] In the United Kingdom, the idea of assured money has been called a "citizen's income."[871] Nobel Prize-winning economist Milton Friedman advocated it in 1962, in the form of a negative income tax.[872] The two key features of Friedman's plan were to allow replacement of what he considered a patchwork of relief agencies and to reduce such a subsidy by amounts earned at work with a sliding scale instead of using the common dollar-for-dollar penalty that forms a solid disincentive to finding a job.[873] During the same decade, economists Robert Theobald, James Tobin, Robert Lampman, and John Kenneth Galbraith proposed similar ideas,[874] and President Lyndon B. Johnson's administration formed a committee, the National Commission on Guaranteed Incomes, which in 1969 issued a report unanimously supporting such a plan.[875] Although a pilot study showed respondents losing little incentive to work,[876] many politicians of the time rejected the idea on those grounds, and it was not implemented.[877] The Earned Income Credit available to low-earning Americans is, however, essentially the same thing in limited form.

Figure 26 summarizes these five guaranteed income ideas.

The Case

Harvard psychology professor Richard J. Herrnstein and American Enterprise Institute fellow Charles Murray argued back in 1994 that if income disparity does not reflect divine will, it is logical to accept some redistribution,[878] and indeed, according to the above precedents, related government programs and payments have been in place for a long time.

If unemployment becomes more and more widespread, those not working will be able to buy fewer and fewer goods and services, thus cutting demand for them and creating a downward

Name	What It Is	Current Examples	Compensation	Points in Favor	Points Against	Prospects
Shadow Wage	Tax benefits for volunteer hours worked	Tax deductions for charitable contributions	The same per hour worked for all people and all tasks	Increases community building at relatively low cost	Doesn't address the problem of disappearing jobs	The lowest cost and least controversial, so the most implementable
Social Wage	Work at government-provided nonprofit jobs	VISTA, Peace Corps, AmeriCorps, and related to workfare	Differ with work and qualifications of worker	Requires fulfilling responsibilities to receive money	Creates bureaucracy and would not replace any government programs	Also implementable if the need is acknowledged
Virtual Jobs	Payments for participating in desired nonwork activities	None, though some similar incentives are appearing in private positions	Differ with amount of education and pay more for gaining further knowledge	Increases a potentially wide range of desirable activities	Problems determining, agreeing upon, and changing what activities qualify	Seems less likely to be enacted than the work-related solutions
Guaranteed-Jobs Constitutional Amendment	Guaranteed work at certain rates of pay, with health insurance or money to cover it	None currently, but related to WPA	The same minimums for all people	Ends unemployment as such	Expensive to require family-supporting pay or would unduly subsidize large families	Doubtful—could seem communistic, and would become progressively more expensive
Citizen's Income	Guaranteed income	Earned Income Credit	The same for all, reduced on a sliding scale by work earnings	Keeps work incentive, streamlines programs, solves income problem	Would be major social change	Relatively extreme, and so could be hard to pass

Figure 26: Comparison of Guaranteed Income Systems

spiral in which poor sales lead to even more layoffs. Of four areas of potential economic limitation— labor, consumer demand, natural resources, and technology—demand might be most likely to be required indefinitely.[879] Therefore, in order to consume, people must have money to spend, and if work won't provide

> ## WORK'S NEW AGE PRINCIPLE #13
>
> **In order for markets to work, people must have money to spend.**

that, they must obtain it somehow.[880] One need only imagine how business owners would react to unemployment vastly higher than 2010's.[881] A solid mean income with a much lower median would cause similar problems, since when earnings increase past certain points, consumption of most products does not follow accordingly; it would be a rare person earning $1 million per year who spent the same share of his income on groceries, electricity, telephone services, and the like as did someone earning $40,000. So for not only mean but median income to increase, we may have to provide it for nonwork activities of some sort.[882]

Another way of seeing the need for guaranteed income is that there have been, historically, three economic subdivisions of work: primary, or extracting raw resources directly through such as farming or mining; secondary, or transforming the resources through manufacturing; and tertiary, through providing other services.[883] America has progressed through its first 100-plus years when most people were employed in the primary sector, through the mid-20th-century peak of secondary work, to the time when a vast majority held service jobs. Mortimer P. Zuckerman wrote that while factories replaced positions lost to farm mechanization, and service work in health care, teaching, and other areas made up for that lost when factories became more productive or left the country, nothing was replacing departing service jobs.[884] The latter are now fading as the others did, so what will replace them? Classic futurist Herman Kahn, forecasting a need beyond 1976, defined such a quaternary sector as "services for their own sake," equated it to leisure, and included in it such activities as religious practices, reading, playing games,

> ## WORK'S NEW AGE PRINCIPLE #14
>
> One person earning $5 million per year does not spend as much on goods and services as 100 people earning $50,000 apiece.

tourism, outdoor recreation, nonvocational skill acquisition and use, and political discussions.[885] Another possibility for the quaternary division is community work.

The requirement for another sector can be seen in how the other three have changed, both in shares of gross national product (GNP) or gross domestic product, depending on which was in use at the time, and in employment. In America in the 1850s, 90% worked in agriculture or associated areas.[886] In 1929, less than 85 years ago, the primary piece included 27.6% of workers and 16.6% of GNP, with the secondary sector at 29.2% and 35.9%, respectively, and tertiary at 43.2% and 46.3%. From that year through 1972, extractive economic activity dropped steadily to 4.8% of both workers and GNP,[887] and by 2008 it employed only 2% of the labor force.[888] Manufacturing reached 34.0% and 36.9% in the wartime year of 1943 and declined thereafter, to 27.8% of workers in 1972[889] and only 6% doing production in early 2011.[890] Services continued to rise, reaching 67.5% of employees and 56.4% of GNP in 1972.[891] In the 40 years since, many service workers have lost their jobs, so what will replace them?

> ## WORK'S NEW AGE PRINCIPLE #15
>
> Factory jobs replaced farm jobs. Service jobs replaced factory jobs. No paid work that we know of now will replace service jobs.

Figure 27 shows the number employed in the primary (extraction), secondary (manufacturing), and tertiary (services) divisions.[892]

If service employment is leveling off or declining, as has been the case for extraction and manufacturing for decades, it is clear that we must introduce a new sector in some form.

None of these guaranteed income ideas may be as expensive as they

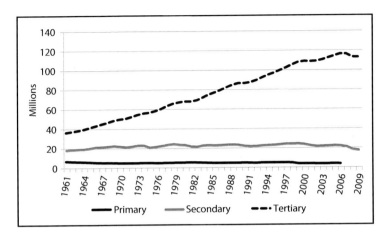

Figure 27: Employment by Primary, Secondary, and Tertiary Work Sectors, 1961–2010

might seem, as they could replace what was estimated early in the 2000s as a cost to the U.S. government of more than $400 billion for each one-point unemployment rate rise.[893] A Value Added Tax (VAT), or one on production or productivity, could replace income taxes to pay for such a program.

Two Things to Decide, and a Decision

In implementing a guaranteed income plan, the first issue we confront is which to choose. The healthiest ones may be those that assure a minimum survival income without controlling further economic activity.[894] To avoid disincentives to work at jobs still available, one critical component of any guaranteed income is that it does not heavily penalize employment earnings. Other countries with such programs have never had large numbers of jobs going unfilled when citizen survival is assured in this way,[895] and tastes for luxuries will see that many people will still vie for work.[896]

The second critical problem would be reaching agreement on how much money, other resources, or end level of prosperity the plan should provide. When politician and sociologist Daniel Patrick Moynihan's 1973 guaranteed income proposal was not

accepted, he charged political liberals with abandoning support over concerns about these specifics.[897] So if America insti-
tutes such a program, what should it deliver? Some writers have
gone quite far in this direction, confusing survival with middle-
class status. Since in many ways prosperity has increased dramatically over the past few decades, let alone over the past century or
since before the Industrial Revolution, it is not reasonable to tie
its definition to the state of others. As for the plan's connection
with work, not only would reducing guaranteed income by the
amount of money otherwise earned strongly discourage people
from doing that, but those in the United States have consistently
shown distaste for equalizing their incomes; in 1992, a study by
The Economist showed 72% of Americans preferring freedom to
equality and 80% against government income-leveling activity,
in great contrast to Germans, of whom on each fewer than 40%
agreed.[898]

Accordingly, I recommend for the United States a citizen's
income set at simple but viable survival levels without subtractions for work, and no-bill, tax-funded universal health care coverage. These programs would end the central problems of Work's
New Age, maintain incentive to do work still existing, and have
much of their cost covered through tax revenue from product
sales and the end of many social welfare programs. As with the
economic stimuli with which the citizen's income would belong,
its final cost could be remarkably low, and a small price to pay
for making a great historical transition as smoothly as reasonably
possible.

Upshot: Do We Have Any Choice?

One problem we could have with any kind of guaranteed
income system is boredom, a theme among those freed from work
in Kurt Vonnegut's now timely *Player Piano*.[899] To that point,
Herman Kahn and others proposed we conceptually follow the
ancient Athenians, who did gymnastics either to prepare for war
or to fight a war.[900] Is there, as Kahn wondered, "something in
the human psyche which requires that the absence of objective

external pressures be balanced by internal psychological structures and goals"?[901] We may find out. In any event, the issue of people having sufficient purpose when divested of personal responsibility for their survival is worthy of serious attention.

Foreseeable problems, though, are not always justifications for rejecting courses of action. We have exceptional reason to see that we need a bold one here. I see no long-term alternative to guaranteed income. While the nation may maintain some prosperity and order for years or even decades with or even without the changes discussed in the last chapter, eventually, as Jeremy Rifkin wrote, it will become clear that "whether a utopian or dystopian future awaits us depends, to a great measure, on how the productivity gains of the Information Age are distributed."[902] This is where we stand. So how can we acclimate ourselves as human beings to the changes we face? That is the subject of Part III.

Part III: Action

Chapter 9:
How Can We Adjust? Changing Our Lives and Our Heads

When we are no longer able to change a situation, we are challenged to change ourselves. —Viktor Frankl[903]

There have been many substantial changes in the United States, and there will soon be more. Whether a guaranteed income program is implemented or not, we will need to adapt in three main areas: our prosperity levels, our attitudes about work in general, and our communities. What changes do we face, and how can we adjust to them?

Adjusting Expectations

Even if many Americans will not have a lot of extra money to spend, the country still offers great advantages. Between 1980 and 2010, life expectancy at birth increased from 78 to 81, with the chance of surviving cancer much higher and the violent crime rate down more than 70%.[904] Since 1970, deaths in motor vehicle crashes have declined by 75%; those in airplane accidents, even more.[905] Computing power bears little resemblance to that of 30 years before.[906] Innumerable consumer products have gone way down in price and up in quality, and many necessities cost far less. In 40 years, dishwashers, central heat, and air conditioning have become much more common, the share of homes without telephones has dropped from 13% to 5%, and 83% have been connected to the Internet.[907] Even with farm subsidies, constant-dollar food costs have declined since 1980.[908] Poverty in America cannot be equated with that in many other countries; although homelessness is a problem, the great majority of poor Americans have, for example, microwave ovens and air conditioning, and almost half own cell phones,[909] while in 2002 about one billion people worldwide were living on around a dollar a day or less.[910]

People will need to make adjustments to having less money, such as cutting spending, saving more, and, if trying to work, accepting variable income.[911] Other possibilities are avoiding debt and considering living with others.[912] Fewer may also own houses, now that the failed overselling of homeownership is over.[913] Altogether, Americans may have to adopt new ideas of what constitutes personal success and failure. The likes of Willy Loman in the Arthur Miller play *Death of a Salesman*, described by *Newsweek* deputy editor Julia Baird as "America's consummate loser," held his job for 38 years, owned his house outright, and had a wife and children,[914] a set of admirable trappings, which, as we have seen, are becoming less and less common. We still have a lot, and we will have more, but it will not be the same as before.

Rethinking Work

The political and social backbone of America and elsewhere in the world has been jobs as we know them.[915] Ulrich Beck stated that "work has become so omnipotent that there is really no other concept opposed to it," and that "a society without work, it seems, is a society without a centre."[916] Author Andre Gorz claimed that jobs were central to the "minds, thoughts and imaginations of everyone" and said that had to change.[917] Yet, as we saw on a small scale in the section about frugal lifestyles, formal employment is not the only way through which human beings can survive[918] or even flourish, and the emotional significance of jobs has already been dropping; the proportion of Americans reporting that they considered work the most important thing in their lives fell from 38% in 1955 to 18% in 1991.[919]

To succeed personally during Work's New Age we, as Jeremy Rifkin put it, will need to "both rethink the very nature of work as well as explore alternative ways human beings might define their role and contribution to society."[920] As he maintained, the loss of many jobs could either mean the end of our civilization or the beginning of something great.[921] We must remember that work as we know it and our current attitudes about it are social constructions[922] that started with the Industrial Revolution,[923] before which many great societies, including our own, prospered. With that history in mind, we can hope that someday unpaid work, or formerly unpaid work compensated through new incentives, will be valued as highly as the other kind and will be as much a font of personal identity.[924]

For all the importance of employment, research has shown that another area provides stronger emotional experiences, that of relationships. The trite line that nobody wishes just before death that he or she had spent more time in the office was verified by caregivers who found that people soon to die usually regretted working as hard as they did and wished instead they had stayed in contact with their friends. Julia Baird wrote, "Having a job is hardly the only, or best, measure of a life."[925] We will have no choice but to take that sentiment seriously in the time to come.

Revaluing Communities

Human groups are valuable, since many life activities from birth to death, including recreation, seeing friends, and much interaction in general happen in them.[926] If people will have considerable free time from not working, they will need activity, which can easily be provided in their communities, in which over the past few decades many functions have been taken out of the hands of locals and given to the federal government.[927] Social capital earned from civic and community activity has many positive characteristics. For example, it can often facilitate easier problem resolution and clear paths toward progress.[928] Local nongovernmental institutions, especially churches, have been historically excellent at providing Americans emergency survival support.

For many who have lost jobs during the past decade, their neighborhoods are especially significant.[929] In smaller towns, a lot of social capital is in evidence; as Richard J. Herrnstein and Charles Murray put it, "Thumb through a few weeks' issues of the newspaper from any small town, and you will find an America that is still replete with fund-raising suppers for the local child who has cancer, drives to collect food and clothing for a family that has suffered a reverse, and even barn raisings."[930] Volunteer organizations have helped with many problems better than others for a long time, their contributions span a vast range from education and entertainment at museums to bargains at church sales, and participating in them has long been part of the American national character.[931] If more community tasks could be reassigned to nongovernmental organizations, they would give opportunities for more local people to contribute to them.[932] Indeed, laws and the free market may prove inadequate to provide as much as they do now, and the motivations behind volunteering, some of which are interpersonal closeness, comradeship, and stewardship, mean it cannot readily be replaced by machines[933] or workers in other countries.

Over the past few years, some have used extra time from unemployment to volunteer more,[934] for which they are compensated informally in social capital instead of financially.[935] A 1992 Gallup poll showed that in the previous year more than half of adult Americans had volunteered somewhere, for an average of 4.2 hours each week and more than 20 billion annually.[936] That same year, there were 1.4 million formal nonprofit organizations[937] with more than half a trillion dollars in assets.[938] Where governmentally staffed and funded service outlets coexist with charitably supported ones, the volunteer ones are often better, in most respects.[939]

High levels of social capital, individually and collectively, correlate strongly with many positive consequences. Children in families and communities where it is substantial have consistently small rates of bad outcomes such as low birth weights and under-age violent crimes, along with better educational results.[940] Adults in states with high social capital are less violent as well[941] and have lower age-adjusted chances of dying.[942] It helps careers directly in many ways, such as by enhancing chances of getting jobs, raises, or promotions.[943] Those with a lot of it tend to fight illnesses better[944] and have superior immune systems, lower blood pressure, and softer arteries.[945] The health correlations with social capital are widespread, to the point where Robert P. Putnam wrote that it could be better medical counsel to call the doctor or anyone else in the morning than to take two aspirin.[946] As well, much research shows that more interpersonally-connected people are also, on average, happier.[947]

Social capital is effective in communities where a volunteer is likely to know others who can help in case of need, but people are increasingly living in densely populated areas and are not in contact with the great majority of others nearby. As a result, it has value limited mostly to those the volunteer knows and may be worthless to others;[948] in effect, social capital is like money that can be spent only at a few stores in one's immediate neighborhood. To improve that, some local groups have turned it into a medium of exchange. One community in Portland, Oregon, had a "time bank," from which people could obtain credits for volunteer hours worked and redeem them for other services.[949] Austin, Texas, had a similar Dillo Trading Club, enhanced by a booklet giving opportunities for Dillo Dollars to be used.[950] Miami's Time Dollar network began in 1983, had an online directory of places to use them, and was mentioned in several scholarly works.[951] New York State's Ithaca Hours began in 1991, had currency printed on paper and tied to dollars, with widespread opportunities to obtain goods as well as services, and distributed notes for more than 10,000 volunteer hours.[952] Brooklyn's

Elderplan HMO used a similar system, including opportunities to exchange currency for medical-related goods, to facilitate its patients helping each other.[953] In 2005, 82 such systems in America were recognized.[954]

What if, Jeremy Rifkin and others have asked, we had a social currency usable all over the country?[955] Such a medium of exchange would be particularly valuable nationwide, as many people, especially those short on money, could trade their resources for those they could not otherwise obtain.[956] Such a national system would serve to formalize the value of volunteer work and thereby to strengthen social capital, a commodity valued all the more in Work's New Age.

Postscript:

Back to Us

Neither a wise man nor a brave man lies down on the tracks of history to wait for the train of the future to run over him. —Dwight D. Eisenhower[957]

Sigmund Freud said the two things necessary for emotional health were "love and work."[958] We strive for one, but what will we do when we cannot realistically obtain the other?

We need something to replace jobs. In 1995, Jeremy Rifkin called that "the critical task ahead for every nation on earth" and wrote that people not needed for employment could either "spell a death sentence for civilization as we know it" or "signal the beginning of a great social transformation, the rebirth of the human spirit."[959] That year, writer Edward Luttwak also pointed out that "most working Americans must rely wholly on their jobs for economic security," making many, even then, seriously insecure.[960] Five years beyond that, Ulrich Beck gave humanity a choice between losing what he called the "work society" or having mass unemployment, with people split between those working and those not.[961] And in 2009, Martin Ford called free-market capitalism a major human innovation, "right up there with the wheel," but he said it plainly could not function without a viable employment market.[962]

I propose an analogue to the progress of physics. Isaac Newton's laws showed us how objects move in the world we experience. A century ago, Albert Einstein's theory of relativity gave us a broader view of how the universe functioned, making Newton's principles not incorrect but a special case, which happened to apply to human beings on Earth but not to objects moving at nearly the speed of light. Soon thereafter, quantum mechanics, still not well understood, had a similar effect on relativity as the latter had on Newton's laws. Newtonian physics is all but 100% valid in the conditions human beings have thus encountered. Relativity is correct with the universe as we understood it a century ago. Quantum mechanics is the best we have right now, but someday it may be likewise superseded. It is probable that laissez-faire capitalism has been the best arrangement thus far, but if we are entering another environment, with arguable root cause the ever-increasing pace of technology, it could now be as ineffective as our gravity is on light beams.

Our ideologies themselves may be as valid now as applying philosophies to the placement of *Titanic* deck chairs—both futile and irrelevant. We in America, the most progressive, innovative, and free-thinking country in the history of the world, need something new. As Gabor Steingart wrote, "Economic growth and social decline are no longer mutually exclusive."[963] Can we follow the example of economist John Maynard Keynes, who said, "If things change, I change my opinion"?[964] Can we accept more modest but more reliably adequate lifestyles, complete with ever-improving health and life expectancy, for most Americans? Can we redefine prosperity to include the cornucopia of free and low-priced resources now generated across the land? Can we continue to improve as a people with far fewer jobs available? Can we have a reasonably objective, level-headed national dialogue on guaranteed income? Are we up to these gargantuan challenges?

In 2010, Julia Baird wrote that the only times Americans felt entitled to "do what they want to do" were when the economy was bad.[965] Other favorable effects of Work's New Age could be for people, as many did when exposed to other living-standard drops early in life in particular, to become more humble, to become kinder, and to expect less.[966] When we react to the employment crisis being much deeper than any economic downturn, we may find a new flowering of choices, gentler but still profound.

Full employment in the United States of America is over. We are in Work's New Age. America, and the lifestyles of Americans, will never be the same. If we maintain the idea that any decent person has the opportunity to work, our nation will be devastated. All that will be left to be determined will be what form that will take—a new feudalism; vast numbers of our countrymen without hope, health, or possessions; those with jobs or especially secure retirements dedicating their resources toward defending themselves from others; companies of all sizes crashing from lack of customers; or worse.

I rest my case with the words of Martin Luther King, Jr.: "We must learn to live together as brothers or perish together as fools."[967]

Endnotes

Introduction: A Shift for the Ages

1   Gorz, Andre (1999), translated by Chris Turner. *Reclaiming Work: Beyond the Wage-Based Society*, p. 1. Cambridge, United Kingdom: Polity Press.

2   Beck, Ulrich (2000), translated by Patrick Camiller. *The Brave New World of Work*, p. 38. Cambridge, United Kingdom: Polity Press.

Chapter 1: Full Employment's End

3   Herbert, Bob, "The Magic Potion," *The New York Times*, March 30, 2010.

4   Beck, *The Brave New World of Work*, pp. 12-13.

5   W. Bridges, cited in Dooley, David and Joann Prause (2004), *The Social Costs of Underemployment: Inadequate Employment as Disguised Unemployment*, p. 7. Cambridge, United Kingdom: Cambridge University Press.

6   Eichengreen, Barry, "Introduction." In Aerts, Erik and Barry Eichengreen (eds.) (1990), *Unemployment and Underemployment in Historical Perspective: Session B-9, Proceedings of Tenth International Economic History Congress, Leuven, August 1990*, p. 9. Leuven, Belgium: Leuven University Press.

7   Ibid., p. 4.

8   Tyler Cowen, cited in Brooks, David, "The Experience Economy," *The New York Times*, February 14, 2011.

9   U.S. Department of Labor, cited in Kaufman, Harold G. (1982), *Professionals in Search of Work: Coping with the Stress of Job Loss and Underemployment*, p. 13. New York: John Wiley & Sons.

10   V. C. Perrella, cited in Kaufman, *Professionals in Search of Work,*
     p. 13.

11   Wikipedia entry on "Industrial Revolution," http://en.wikipedia.
     org/wiki/Industrial_Revolution.

12   Rifkin, Jeremy (2004). *The End of Work: The Decline of the
     Global Labor Force and the Dawn of the Post-Market Era,* pp.
     64-65. New York: Jeremy P. Tarcher / Penguin.

13   Ibid., p. 81.

14   Wikipedia entry on "1973 Oil Crisis," http://en.wikipedia.org/
     wiki/1973_oil_crisis.

15   Lakshman Achuthan, cited in Goodman, Peter S., "The New
     Poor: Millions of Unemployed Face Years Without Jobs," *The
     New York Times,* February 21, 2010.

16   Zuckerman, Mortimer B., "Unemployment Rate is Worse Than
     it Looks," *U.S. News & World Report,* August 20, 2010.

17   Ryan, Mary Meghan (ed.), (2009). *Handbook of U.S. Labor Sta-
     tistics: Employment, Earnings, Prices, Productivity, and Other
     Labor Data* (12th ed.), p. 9. Lanham, MD: Bernan Press; Bureau
     of Labor Statistics.

18   Friedman, Thomas L. (2007). *The World Is Flat: A Brief History
     of the Twenty-First Century* (Release 3.0), p. 138. New York: Pica-
     dor/Farrar, Straus, and Giroux.

19   Ibid., p. 60.

20   Ibid., p. 111.

21   Peck, Don, "How a New Jobless Era Will Transform America,"
     The Atlantic, March 2010.

22   Newman, Rick, "Why Politicians Can't Create Real Jobs," *U.S.
     News & World Report,* February 16, 2010.

23   Peck, "How a New Jobless Era Will Transform America."

24   Meyerson, Harold, "Corporate America, Paving a Downward
     Economic Slide," *The Washington Post,* January 5, 2011.

25   Zuckerman, "Unemployment Rate is Worse Than it Looks."

26   Indiviglio, Daniel, "42 States Had Fewer Employed Workers in
     August," *The Atlantic,* September 2010.

27   Goodman, "The New Poor"; Silverblatt, Rob, "Why the Unem-
     ployment Rate Refuses to Budge," *U.S. News & World Report,*
     April 2, 2010; Hauser, Christine, "Private Sector Improves Jobs
     Picture Only Moderately," *The New York Times,* January 7, 2011;
     Peck, "How a New Jobless Era Will Transform America"; Wolge-
     muth, Liz, "Why the December Jobs Report Is Such a Bust," *U.S.*

News & World Report, January 8, 2010; Rich, Motoko, "Few New Jobs as Jobless Rate Rises to 9.8%," *The New York Times,* December 3, 2010.

28 Hauser, "Private Sector Improves Jobs Picture Only Moderately."

29 Zuckerman, Mortimer B., "The Jobless Recovery Remains Issue Number One," *U.S. News & World Report,* May 28, 2010.

30 Rampell, Catherine, "Comparing Recoveries: Job Changes," Economix blog, *The New York Times,* January 7, 2011, http://economix.blogs.nytimes.com/.

31 "The Economy in 2011," *The New York Times, January 1, 2011.*

32 Bureau of Labor Statistics.

33 Zuckerman, Mortimer B., "Obama's Healthcare Focus Is Misguided," *U.S. News & World Report, March 12, 2010.*

34 Ryan, *Handbook of U.S. Labor Statistics,* p. 4.

35 Ibid., pp. 4-5.

36 Ryan, *Handbook of U.S. Labor Statistics,* p. 83; Bureau of Labor Statistics.

37 Ryan, *Handbook of U.S. Labor Statistics,* pp. 9, 92; Bureau of Labor Statistics.

38 Ryan, *Handbook of U.S. Labor Statistics,* p. 103; Bureau of Labor Statistics.

39 Calculated from Ryan, *Handbook of U.S. Labor Statistics,* pp. 83, 103; Bureau of Labor Statistics.

40 Ryan, *Handbook of U.S. Labor Statistics,* p. 5.

41 Economic Policy Institute, cited in Rifkin, *The End of Work,* p. xvi.

42 Wolgemuth, Liz, "What a 9.7 Percent Unemployment Rate Means," *U.S. News & World Report,* February 5, 2010.

43 Rich, "Few New Jobs as Jobless Rate Rises to 9.8%."

44 David Leonhardt, cited in Rifkin, *The End of Work,* p. xvi.

45 Bureau of Labor Statistics.

46 Epstein, Gene (2006). *Econospinning: How to Read Between the Lines When the Media Manipulate the Numbers,* p. 66. New York: John Wiley & Sons, Inc.

47 Ibid., p. 70.

48 Clogg, Clifford C. (1979). *Measuring Underemployment,* p. 3. New York: Academic Press.

49 P. M. Hauser, cited in Clogg, *Measuring Underemployment,* pp. 9-10.

50 March Current Population Survey, cited in Clogg, *Measuring Underemployment,* pp. 22-23.

51 Clifford C. Clogg, cited in Clogg, Clifford C., Eliason, R. Scott, and Kevin T. Leicht (2001), *Analyzing the Labor Force: Concepts, Measures, and Trends,* p. 47. New York: Kluwer Academic/Plenum Publishers.

52 Ibid., p. 51.

53 R. P. Quinn and G. L. Staines, cited in Clogg, Eliason, and Leicht, *Analyzing the Labor Force,* p. 77.

54 Kaufman, *Professionals in Search of Work,* p. 13.

55 Friedman, *The World Is Flat,* p. 268.

56 U.S. Department of Labor, cited in Kaufman, *Professionals in Search of Work,* p. 14.

57 R. Freeman, cited in Clogg, Eliason, and Leicht, *Analyzing the Labor Force,* p. 48.

58 Ryan, *Handbook of U.S. Labor Statistics,* p. 140. The trend line is not shown, as it is very close to the actual data.

59 Kaufman, *Professionals in Search of Work,* p. 224.

60 Ibid., pp. 224-225.

61 Ryan, *Handbook of U.S. Labor Statistics,* p. 4.

62 Bureau of Labor Statistics.

63 Ryan, *Handbook of U.S. Labor Statistics,* p. 5.

64 Newman, Rick, "An Unseen Economic Albatross: Labor-Force Dropouts," *U.S. News & World Report,* January 8, 2010.

65 Ryan, *Handbook of U.S. Labor Statistics,* p. 51; Bureau of Labor Statistics.

66 Ryan, *Handbook of U.S. Labor Statistics,* p. 51.

67 Ryan, *Handbook of U.S. Labor Statistics,* p. 51; Bureau of Labor Statistics.

68 Ryan, *Handbook of U.S. Labor Statistics,* p. 51.

69 Ibid., p. 5.

70 Ryan, *Handbook of U.S. Labor Statistics,* p. 51; Bureau of Labor Statistics.

71 Ryan, *Handbook of U.S. Labor Statistics,* p. 5.

72 Ryan, *Handbook of U.S. Labor Statistics,* p. 51; Bureau of Labor Statistics.

73 Ryan, *Handbook of U.S. Labor Statistics,* p. 51.

74 Ryan, *Handbook of U.S. Labor Statistics,* p. 51; Bureau of Labor Statistics.

75 Ryan, *Handbook of U.S. Labor Statistics,* p. 5.

76 U.S. Census Bureau.

77 Ryan, *Handbook of U.S. Labor Statistics,* p. 4.

78 U.S. Census Bureau.

79 Tolson, Jay, "A Growing Trend of Leaving America," *U.S. News & World Report,* July 28, 2008.

80 Association of Americans Resident Overseas website, www.aaro.org.

81 Tolson, "A Growing Trend of Leaving America."

82 Wolgemuth, "Why the December Jobs Report Is Such a Bust."

83 Rich, Motoko, "A Jobless Rate Still Unaffected by New Hiring," *The New York Times,* June 3, 2010.

84 Orszag, Peter, "Making Disability Work," *The New York Times,* December 9, 2010.

85 Will, George F., "Democrats Vs. Wal-Mart," *The Washington Post,* September 14, 2006.

86 Bureau of Labor Statistics.

87 Will, "Democrats Vs. Wal-Mart."

88 Thoma, Mark, "The Technology Factor," Room for Debate blog, *The New York Times,* January 17, 2011, http://www.nytimes.com/roomfordebate.

89 Newman, "An Unseen Economic Albatross."

90 Ryan, *Handbook of U.S. Labor Statistics,* pp. 9, 48, 52; Calculated from U.S. Census Bureau.

91 "February's Jobs Report," *The New York Times,* March 4, 2011.

92 "Fed Boss: It Will Take Years for Jobs to Come Back," *U.S. News & World Report,* January 7, 2011.

93 Zuckerman, Mortimer P., "The American Jobs Machine is Clanging to a Halt," *U.S. News & World Report,* October 1, 2010.

94 Zuckerman, Mortimer P., "The Great Jobs Recession Goes On," *U.S. News & World Report,* February 11, 2011.

95 Johnson, Simon, "Employment vs. Corporate Profit," Room for Debate blog, *The New York Times,* January 17, 2011, http://www.nytimes.com/roomfordebate.

96 Samuelson, Robert J., "The Big Hiring Freeze," *Newsweek,* July 23, 2010.

97 Toles, Tom, "Works For Him," *The Washington Post,* November 28, 2010.

98 Toles, Tom, "Shape of Things to Come," *The Washington Post,* February 22, 2011.

99 Skandalaris, Bob (2006). *Rebuilding the American Dream: Restoring American Jobs and Competitiveness Through Innovation and Entrepreneurship,* p. 2. Bloomfield Hills, MI: Pembrook Publishing.

100 Zuckerman, "Unemployment Rate Is Worse Than It Looks."

101 Skandalaris, *Rebuilding the American Dream,* p. 2.

102 Zuckerman, "Unemployment Rate Is Worse Than It Looks."

103 Samuelson, Robert J., "The Age of Austerity," *The Washington Post,* October 11, 2010.

104 Luce, von Edward, "Das Ende des amerikanische Traums," *Financial Times Deutschland,* August 9, 2010.

105 Herbert, Bob, "Hiding From Reality," *The New York Times,* November 19, 2010.

106 Beck, *The Brave New World of Work,* p. 2.

107 Karabell, Zachary, "We Are Not In This Together," *Newsweek,* April 11, 2009.

Chapter 2: It'll Get Worse

108 Meyerson, Harold, "Where's the Economic Recovery?," *The Washington Post,* March 9, 2011.

109 Rifkin, *The End of Work,* p. xiv.

110 Ford, Martin (2009), *The Lights in the Tunnel: Automation, Accelerating Technology, and the Economy of the Future,* pp. 112. Acculant Publishing.

111 Levy, Frank and Richard J. Murnane (2004). *The New Division of Labor: How Computers Are Creating the Next Job Market,* p. 1. Princeton, NJ: Princeton University Press.

112 Robert MacBride, cited in Rifkin, *The End of Work,* p. 82.

113 David Noble, cited in Rifkin, *The End of Work,* p. 84.

114 Levy and Murnane, *The New Division of Labor,* pp. 3, 35.

115 Ibid., p. 37.

116 Rifkin, *The End of Work,* p. 6.

117 Levy and Murnane, *The New Division of Labor,* p. 36.

118 Cited in Rifkin, *The End of Work,* p. 8.

119 Rifkin, *The End of Work,* pp. 3, 5.

120 See Rifkin, *The End of Work,* pp. 129-162.

121 U.S. Department of Labor, cited in Rifkin, *The End of Work,* p. 167.

122 Levy and Murnane, *The New Division of Labor,* pp. 35, 42.

123 Ibid., p. 2.

124 Ron Hira and Anil Hira, cited in Skandalaris, *Rebuilding the American Dream,* p. 17.

125 Pelton, Joseph N. and Marshall, Peter (2010). *MegaCrunch!: Ten Survival Strategies for 21st Century Challenges,* p. 44. Bethesda, MD: PMAssociates.

126 Ibid., p. 44.

127 Ibid., p. 45.

128 Skandalaris, *Rebuilding the American Dream,* p. 18.

129 Pelton and Marshall, *MegaCrunch!,* p. 45.

130 Bureau of Labor Statistics, cited in Ford, *The Lights in the Tunnel,* p. 60.

131 Markoff, John, "Armies of Expensive Lawyers, Replaced by Cheaper Software," *The New York Times,* March 4, 2011.

132 Shin, Hyon-hee, "Robotic Helpers Coming to Homes, Offices," *The Korea Herald,* January 19, 2011.

133 Zuckerman, "The American Jobs Machine Is Clanging to a Halt."

134 Rifkin, *The End of Work,* p. 5.

135 Zuckerman, "The Great Jobs Recession Goes On."

136 Ford, *The Lights in the Tunnel,* p. 3.

137 Pelton and Marshall, *MegaCrunch!,* p. 7.

138 Ford, *The Lights in the Tunnel,* p. 64.

139 Ibid., pp. 72-73.

140 Rifkin, *The End of Work,* p. xxii; Ford, Martin, "What If There's No Fix for High Unemployment?", CNNMoney.com, June 10, 2010, http://money.cnn.com/.

141 Friedman, *The World Is Flat,* p. 273.

142 Rifkin, *The End of Work,* p. 289.

143 Brooks, "The Experience Economy."

144 Ford, The Lights in the Tunnel, pp. 9, 67.

145 Rifkin, *The End of Work,* p. xviii.

146 Levy and Murnane, *The New Division of Labor,* p.13.

147 David Autor, Frank Levy, and Richard Murnane, cited in Krugman, Paul, "Degrees and Dollars," *The New York Times,* March 6, 2011.

148 Schaeffer, Jonathan et al., "Checkers is Solved," *Science,* September 14, 2007.

149 Ford, *The Lights in the Tunnel,* p. 71.

150 Levy and Murnane, *The New Division of Labor,* p. 7.

151 Ford, *The Lights in the Tunnel,* p. 64.

152 Ibid., p. 80.

153 Ibid., p. 66.

154 Ibid., p. 77.

155 Ibid., p. 75.

156 Skandalaris, *Rebuilding the American Dream,* p. 17.

157 Levy and Murnane, *The New Division of Labor,* p. 14.

158 Vonnegut Jr., Kurt (1952). *Player Piano,* p. 199. New York: Avon Books.

159 Ford, *The Lights in the Tunnel,* p. 92.

160 Kurzweil, Ray (2005). *The Singularity is Near: When Humans Transcend Biology,* p. 8. New York: Penguin Books.

161 Ibid., pp. 9, 136.

162 Google Finance, cited in Ford, *The Lights in the Tunnel,* p. 133.

163 Ford, *The Lights in the Tunnel,* p. 221.

164 Google Finance, cited in Ford, *The Lights in the Tunnel,* p. 133.

165 Ford, *The Lights in the Tunnel,* p. 133.

166 Ibid., p. 95.

167 Ibid., pp. 212, 226.

168 Ford, "What If There's No Fix for High Unemployment?"

169 Murray, John E. (2007). *Origins of American Health Insurance: A History of Industrial Sickness Funds,* p. 3. New Haven, CT: Yale University Press.

170 Ibid., p. 65.

171 Ohio Health and Old Age Insurance Commission, cited in Murray, *Origins of American Health Insurance,* p. 42.

172 Mahar, Maggie (2006). *Money-Driven Medicine: The Real Reason Health Care Costs So Much,* p. 7. New York: HarperCollins Publishers.

173 Ibid., pp. 8-9.

174 Paul Starr, cited in Bodenheimer, Thomas S. and Grumbach, Kevin (2002), *Understanding Health Policy: A Clinical Approach,* p. 8. New York: McGraw-Hill.

175 Mahar, *Money-Driven Medicine,* p. 10.

176 Paul Starr, cited in Mahar, *Money-Driven Medicine,* p. 10.

177 Murray, *Origins of American Health Insurance,* p. 235.

178 Odin W. Anderson and Jacob J. Feldman, cited in Mahar, *Money-Driven Medicine,* p. 10.

179 Mahar, *Money-Driven Medicine,* p. 27.

180 James C. Robinson, cited in Mahar, *Money-Driven Medicine,* pp. 10-11.

181 Mahar, *Money-Driven Medicine,* p. 12.

182 Howard Wolinsky and Tom Brune, cited in Mahar, *Money-Driven Medicine,* p. 12.

183 Mahar, *Money-Driven Medicine,* p. 15.

184 James C. Robinson, cited in Mahar, *Money-Driven Medicine,* p. 17.

185 G. Anderson and P. S. Hussey, cited in Bodenheimer and Grumbach, *Understanding Health Policy,* p. 173.

186 Alice M. Rivlin, cited in Mahar, *Money-Driven Medicine,* p. 18.

187 Mahar, *Money-Driven Medicine,* p. 19.

188 James C. Robinson, cited in Mahar, *Money-Driven Medicine,* p. 22.

189 G. Anderson and P. S. Hussey, cited in Bodenheimer and Grumbach, *Understanding Health Policy,* p. 173

190 Mahar, *Money-Driven Medicine,* p. 24.

191 Lynn R. Gruber, Maureen Shadle, and Cynthia L. Polich, cited in Mahar, *Money-Driven Medicine,* p. 23.

192 L. Bergthold, cited in Bodenheimer and Grumbach, *Understanding Health Policy,* p. 188.

193 J. C. Cantor et al., cited in Bodenheimer and Grumbach, *Understanding Health Policy,* p. 188.

194 G. Anderson and P. S. Hussey, cited in Bodenheimer and Grumbach, *Understanding Health Policy,* p. 173.

195 Mahar, *Money-Driven Medicine,* p. 27.

196 InterStudy, cited in Gray, Bradford H., "The Rise and Decline of the HMO: A Chapter in U.S. Health Policy History." In Stevens,

Rosemary A., Charles E. Rosenberg, and Lawton R. Burns (eds.), (2006), *History & Health Policy in the United States,* p. 312. New Brunswick, New Jersey: Rutgers University Press.

197 Cutler, David M. (2004), *Your Money or Your Life: Strong Medicine for America's Healthcare System,* pp. 87-88. New York: Oxford University Press, Inc.

198 Bodenheimer and Grumbach, *Understanding Health Policy,* p. 189.

199 Ibid., p. 13.

200 G. Anderson and P. S. Hussey, cited in Bodenheimer and Grumbach, *Understanding Health Policy,* p. 173

201 Bodenheimer and Grumbach, *Understanding Health Policy,* p. 113.

202 The Washington Post (2010). *Landmark: The Inside Story of America's New Health-Care Law and What It Means for Us All,* p. 101. Philadelphia: PublicAffairs.

203 The Henry J. Kaiser Family Foundation, cited in Mahar, *Money-Driven Medicine,* p. 34.

204 Paul B. Ginsburg, Bradley C. Strunk, Michelle I. Banker, and John P. Cookson, cited in Eibner, Christine (2008), *The Economic Burden of Providing Health Insurance: How Much Worse Off Are Small Firms?,* p. 1. Santa Monica, CA: The RAND Corporation.

205 Agency for Healthcare Research and Quality, cited in Eibner, *The Economic Burden of Providing Health Insurance,* p. 1.

206 Eibner, *The Economic Burden of Providing Health Insurance,* p. 37.

207 Mahar, *Money-Driven Medicine,* pp. 7, 27.

208 Cohen, Richard, "Boehner's Health Delusion," *The Washington Post,* November 9, 2010.

209 Hoffman, G.L., "Why Are Companies Sitting on Cash But Not Hiring?", *U.S. News & World Report,* September 7, 2010.

210 Mont, Joe, "Health Costs Seen Hitting Five-Year High," *Newsweek,* September 29, 2010.

211 Ibid.

212 Eibner, *The Economic Burden of Providing Health Insurance,* p. 41.

213 Zuckerman, "The American Jobs Machine is Clanging to a Halt."

214 Thompson, Derek, "The Four Horsemen of the Job-Pocalypse," *The Atlantic,* August 2010.

215 The Washington Post, *Landmark,* pp. 153-154.

216 Ibid., pp. 155-156.

217 Ibid., pp. 156-157.

218 Ibid., p. 157.

219 Ibid., pp. 157-158.

220 Ibid., pp. 160-161.

221 Rifkin, *The End of Work,* p. 96.

222 James Womack, Daniel Jones, and Daniel Roos, cited in Rifkin, *The End of Work,* p. 96.

223 Wallulis, Jerald (1998). *The New Insecurity: The End of the Standard Job and Family,* p. 96. Albany, NY: State University of New York Press.

224 Ibid., p. 97.

225 Thoma, "The Technology Factor."

226 Cowen, Tyler, "Some Jobs Aren't Needed," Room for Debate blog, *The New York Times,* January 17, 2011, http://www.nytimes.com/roomfordebate.

227 Wallulis, *The New Insecurity,* p. xiv.

228 Ibid.

229 Louis Uchitelle, cited in Rifkin, *The End of Work,* p. xv.

230 National Employment Law Project, cited in Meyerson, "Where's the Economic Recovery?"

231 Zuckerman, "The Great Jobs Recession Goes On."

232 Mishel, Lawrence, Jared Bernstein, and Heidi Shierholz (2009). *The State of Working America 2008/2009,* p. 149. Ithaca, NY: ILR Press.

233 Ibid., p. 150.

234 The Henry J. Kaiser Family Foundation, cited in Mahar, *Money-Driven Medicine,* p. xiv.

235 Bandyk, Matthew, "Fewer Employees, Higher Health Insurance Costs," *U.S. News & World Report,* June 16, 2008.

236 Brandon, Emily, "Fewer Workers Enrolled in 401(k)s," *U.S. News & World Report,* March 26, 2010.

237 Cook, Nancy, "Are Fed-Up American Workers Getting Their Gumption Back?", *Newsweek,* August 6, 2010.

238 Beck, *The Brave New World of Work,* p. 114.

239 John M. Berry and Mike Allen, cited in Rifkin, *The End of Work,* p. xvi.

240 Harwood, John, "Mystery for White House: Where Did the Jobs Go?", The Caucus blog, *The New York Times,* July 19, 2010, http://thecaucus.blogs.nytimes.com/.

241 Meyerson, "Where's the Economic Recovery?"

242 Cook, "Are Fed-Up American Workers Getting Their Gumption Back?"

243 Foroohar, Rana, "You Call This a Recovery?", *Newsweek,* August 7, 2010.

244 Zuckerman, "The Jobless Recovery Remains Issue Number One."

245 Gross, Daniel, "We're Mad as Hell!", *Newsweek,* August 15, 2010.

246 Calculated from Ryan, *Handbook of U.S. Labor Statistics,* p. 258; Bureau of Labor Statistics.

247 Ryan, *Handbook of U.S. Labor Statistics,* p. 256.

248 Zuckerman, "The Jobless Recovery Remains Issue Number One."

249 *The Wall Street Journal,* cited in Gross, "We're Mad as Hell!"

250 Pearlstein, Steven, "Wage Cuts Hurt, But They May Be the Only Way to Get Americans Back to Work," *The Washington Post,* October 12, 2010.

251 U.S. Department of Labor, Bureau of Labor Statistics News Release, July 27, 2010, http://www.bls.gov/news.release/pdf/ebs2.pdf.

252 Truman Bewley, cited in Shiller, Robert J. "The Survival of the Safest," *The New York Times,* October 2, 2010.

253 Pearlstein, "Wage Cuts Hurt, But They May Be the Only Way to Get Americans Back to Work."

254 Shiller, "The Survival of the Safest."

255 Cook, "Are Fed-Up American Workers Getting Their Gumption Back?"; Gross, "We're Mad as Hell!"

256 Gross, "We're Mad as Hell!"

257 Cook, "Are Fed-Up American Workers Getting Their Gumption Back?"

258 For example, see Friedman, George (2009), *The Next 100 Years: A Forecast for the 21st Century,* p. 132. New York: Anchor Books.

259 See Huntington, James B. (2007), *Prospects for Increased Post-65 Career Employment for the Baby Boom Generation,* pp. 41-43. Ann Arbor, MI: ProQuest Information and Learning Company.

260 Dychtwald, Ken, and Joe Flower (1990). *Age Wave: The Challenges and Opportunities of an Aging America,* p. 176. New York: Bantam Books.

261 Arnott, Robert D., and Anne Cascells, "Will We Retire Later and Poorer?", *Journal of Investing,* 2004.

262 Huntington, *Prospects for Increased Post-65 Career Employment for the Baby Boom Generation,* p. 1.

263 U.S. Census Bureau (2005). *Statistical Abstract of the United States: 2006* (125th ed.), p. 450. Washington, DC: U.S. Government Printing Office.

264 Purcell, Patrick. J., "Retirement Savings and Household Wealth: A Summary of Recent Data," *Journal of Pension Planning & Compliance,* 2004.

265 Huntington, *Prospects for Increased Post-65 Career Employment for the Baby Boom Generation, p. 120.*

266 Newman, Rick, "Why Baby Boomers Are Bummed Out," *U.S. News & World Report,* December 29, 2010.

267 Ted Fishman, cited in Brandon, Emily, "The Baby Boomers Turn 65," *U.S. News & World Report,* December 20, 2010.

268 Brandon, "The Baby Boomers Turn 65."

269 Newman, "Why Baby Boomers Are Bummed Out."

270 Newman, Rick, "New Rules for a Darwinian Economy," *U.S. News & World Report,* January 19, 2010.

271 Wellner, Alison Stein, "Tapping a Silver Mine," HR Magazine, March 2002.

272 AARP (2004). *Baby Boomers Envision Retirement II: Survey of Baby Boomers' Expectations for Retirement.* Washington, DC, http://www.aarp.org/research/work/employment/.

273 Cutler, Neal E., "Hale & Hearty: Healthy Older-Age Life Expectancy in the 21st Century," *Journal of Financial Service Professionals,* 2005.

274 Bovbjerg, Barbara D. (2005). *Redefining Retirement: Options for Older Americans* (GAO report GAO-05-620T), p. 4. Washington, DC: U.S. Government Printing Office.

275 Dychtwald, Ken, "Ageless Aging: The Next Era of Retirement," *Futurist,* July/August 2005.

276 Ryan, *Handbook of U.S. Labor Statistics,* p. 228; Bureau of Labor Statistics.

277 Dychtwald, "Ageless Aging."

278 http://www.cdc.gov/nchs/data/hus/hus10.pdf#022.

279 Ford, *The Lights in the Tunnel,* p. 214.

280 See Samuelson, Robert J., "The Mystery of Stubborn Unemployment," *Newsweek,* October 8, 2010.

281 Zuckerman, "Unemployment Rate is Worse Than it Looks."

282 Samuelson, "The Mystery of Stubborn Unemployment."

283 Krugman, Paul, "Structure of Excuses," *The New York Times,* September 26, 2010

284 Cited in Krugman, "Structure of Excuses."

285 Pearlstein, Steven, "The Bleak Truth About Unemployment," *The Washington Post,* September 7, 2010.

286 Indeed career website, "Job Market Competition," www.indeed.com/jobtrends/unemployment.

287 Pearlstein, "The Bleak Truth About Unemployment."

288 Cited in Gunn, Dwyer, "Betsey Stevenson Answers Your Questions," Freakonomics blog, October 13, 2010, http://www.freakonomics.com/blog/; Zuckerman, "The American Jobs Machine is Clanging to a Halt"; Foroohar, Rana, "Where the Jobs Are," *Newsweek,* September 25, 2010.

289 Samuelson, "The Mystery of Stubborn Unemployment."

290 Krugman, "Structure of Excuses."

291 Cited in Gunn, "Betsey Stevenson Answers Your Questions."

292 Krugman, "Structure of Excuses."

293 Ibid.

294 Thompson, Derek, "CBO Counters Liberals: There Is Some Structural Unemployment," *The Atlantic,* September 2010.

295 Zuckerman, "The American Jobs Machine is Clanging to a Halt."

296 Capital Economics, cited in Foroohar, "Where the Jobs Are."

297 Harwood, "Mystery for White House."

298 Samuelson, "The Mystery of Stubborn Unemployment."

299 Thompson, "The Four Horsemen of the Job-Pocalypse."

300 Samuelson, "The Mystery of Stubborn Unemployment."

301 McArdle, Megan, "What to Do About Long-Term Unemployment?" *The Atlantic,* March 2010.

302 Green, Alison, "10 Mistakes Employers Make in Hiring," *U.S. News & World Report,* July 21, 2008.

303 Shapiro, Cynthia (2008). *What Does Somebody Have to Do to Get a Job Around Here?*, p. 192. New York: St. Martin's Press.

304 Tom G. Palmer, cited in Wikipedia entry on "Globalization," http://en.wikipedia.org/wiki/Globalization.

305 Cited in Steingart, Gabor (2008), *The War for Wealth: The True Story of Globalization, or Why the Flat World is Broken*, p. 2. New York: McGraw-Hill.

306 Newman, Rick, "5 Reasons Companies Still Aren't Hiring," *U.S. News & World Report*, August 10, 2010.

307 Steingart, *The War for Wealth*, p. 149.

308 Friedman, *The World Is Flat*, p. 25.

309 Newman, "Why Politicians Can't Create Real Jobs."

310 Peck, "How a New Jobless Era Will Transform America."

311 Karabell, Zachary (2010), *Superfusion: How China and America Became One Economy and Why the World's Prosperity Depends on It*, p. 49. New York: Simon & Schuster Paperbacks.

312 Meyerson, "Corporate America, Paving a Downward Economic Slide."

313 Zuckerman, "The American Jobs Machine is Clanging to a Halt."

314 Andy Grove, cited in Zuckerman, "The American Jobs Machine is Clanging to a Halt."

315 Foroohar, Rana, "Joblessness is Here to Stay," Newsweek, December 12, 2009.

316 Peck, "How a New Jobless Era Will Transform America."

317 Steingart, *The War for Wealth*, pp. 11-12.

318 Cited in Steingart, *The War for Wealth*, p. 135.

319 McKinsey Global Institute, cited in Foroohar, "Joblessness is Here to Stay."

320 Cited in Steingart, *The War for Wealth*, p. 201.

321 Foroohar, "Joblessness is Here to Stay."

322 Ford, *The Lights in the Tunnel*, p. 86.

323 Ibid., p. 87.

324 Friedman, *The World Is Flat*, p. 280.

325 Rich, Motoko and Jack Ewing, "Weaker Dollar Seen as Unlikely to Cure Unemployment," *The New York Times*, November 15, 2010.

326 Cited in Rich and Ewing, "Weaker Dollar Seen as Unlikely to Cure Unemployment."

327 Steve Blitz, cited in Rich and Ewing, "Weaker Dollar Seen as Unlikely to Cure Unemployment."

328 Rich and Ewing, "Weaker Dollar Seen as Unlikely to Cure Unemployment."

329 Nigel Gault, cited in Rich and Ewing, "Weaker Dollar Seen as Unlikely to Cure Unemployment."

330 Ford, *The Lights in the Tunnel*, p. 55.

331 Rifkin, *The End of Work*, p. 291.

332 Ford, *The Lights in the Tunnel*, p. 113.

333 "Lay Off the Layoffs," *Newsweek*, February 5, 2010.

334 Wayne Cascio, cited in "Lay Off the Layoffs."

335 "Lay Off the Layoffs."

336 Wayne Cascio, cited in "Lay Off the Layoffs."

337 American Management Association, cited in "Lay Off the Layoffs."

338 *The New York Times*, cited in Wallulis, *The New Insecurity*, p. 84.

339 Ford, "What If There's No Fix for High Unemployment?"

340 Newman, "Why Politicians Can't Create Real Jobs."

341 Heather Boushey, cited in "Can Obama Create More Jobs Soon?"

342 Cited in Beck, *The Brave New World of Work*, p. 62.

Chapter 3: The Effects, So Far and Soon

343 Wilson, William Julius (1996). *When Work Disappears: The World of the New Urban Poor*, p. 78. New York: Vintage Books.

344 Peck, "How a New Jobless Era Will Transform America."

345 Sheehy, Gail (1995). *New Passages: Mapping Your Life Against Time*, p. 3. New York: Random House.

346 Sørensen, Aage B. (1998). "Career Trajectories and the Older Worker." In K. Schaie and C. Schooler (eds.), *Impact of Work on Older Adults*, p. 207. New York: Springer Publishing Company, Inc.

347 Charles Handy, cited in Wallulis, *The New Insecurity*, p. 105.

348 Wallulis, *The New Insecurity*, p. 167.

349 Peck, "How a New Jobless Era Will Transform America."

350 Henig, Robin Marantz, "What Is It About 20-Somethings?", *The New York Times*, August 18, 2010.

351 Arnett, Jeffrey Jensen (2007). *Adolescence and Emerging Adulthood: A Cultural Approach* (3rd ed.), p. 7. Upper Saddle River, NJ: Pearson Education, Inc.

352 S. F. Hamilton and M. A. Hamilton, cited in Arnett, *Adolescence and Emerging Adulthood,* pp. 376-377.

353 P. C. Glick, cited in Mitchell, Barbara (2006), *The Boomerang Age: Transitions to Adulthood in Families,* p. 42. New Brunswick, NJ: Transaction Publishers.

354 A. Cherlin, cited in Mitchell, *The Boomerang Age,* p. 43.

355 Ibid., p. 42.

356 R. M. Kreider and J. M. Fields, cited in Mitchell, *The Boomerang Age,* p. 52.

357 U.S. Bureau of the Census, cited in Arnett, *Adolescence and Emerging Adulthood,* p. 16.

358 Henig, "What Is It About 20-Somethings?"

359 Cohen, Patricia, "Long Road to Adulthood is Growing Even Longer," *The New York Times,* June 11, 2010.

360 F. Goldscheider and C. Goldscheider, cited in Mitchell, *The Boomerang Age*, p. 41.

361 F. Goldscheider, cited in Mitchell, *The Boomerang Age,* p. 45.

362 Mitchell, *The Boomerang Age,* p. 45.

363 Peck, "How a New Jobless Era Will Transform America."

364 Cohen, "Long Road to Adulthood is Growing Even Longer."

365 F. Goldscheider and C. Goldscheider, cited in Mitchell, *The Boomerang Age,* p. 76.

366 Pew survey, cited in Peck, "How a New Jobless Era Will Transform America."

367 Henig, "What Is It About 20-Somethings?"

368 United States Census Bureau, cited in Henig, "What Is It About 20-Somethings?"

369 Peck, "How a New Jobless Era Will Transform America."

370 Wiener, Valerie (1997). *The Nesting Syndrome: Grown Children Living at Home,* p. 61. Minneapolis, MN: Fairview Press.

371 F. Goldscheider and C. Goldscheider, cited in Mitchell, *The Boomerang Age,* p. 68.

372 M. Boyd, cited in Mitchell, *The Boomerang Age,* p. 70.

373 F. Goldscheider and C. Goldscheider, cited in Mitchell, *The Boomerang Age,* p. 70

374 Sheehy, *New Passages,* pp. 48-49.

375 Cook, Nancy, "The Workers of the Future," *Newsweek,* February 26, 2010.

376 Peck, "How a New Jobless Era Will Transform America."

377 Samuelson, Robert J., "The Real Generation Gap," *Newsweek,* March 5, 2010.

378 Ryan, *Handbook of U.S. Labor Statistics,* p. 107.

379 Henig, "What Is It About 20-Somethings?"

380 Wallulis, *The New Insecurity,* p. 191.

381 Romano, Andrew, "Why Insuring Young Adults Until They Turn 26 Is Good for the Rest of Us," *Newsweek,* April 27, 2010.

382 "February's Jobs Report."

383 Calculated from Ryan, *Handbook of U.S. Labor Statistics,* pp. 30, 39; Bureau of Labor Statistics.

384 Cohen, "Long Road to Adulthood is Growing Even Longer."

385 Henig, "What Is It About 20-Somethings?"

386 Jeffrey Jensen Arnett, cited in Arnett, *Adolescence and Emerging Adulthood,* p. 15.

387 Bird, Caroline (1975), *The Case Against College,* pp. 3-4. New York: David McKay Company, Inc.

388 Henig, "What Is It About 20-Somethings?"

389 Ibid.

390 Arnett, Jeffrey Jensen (2004). *Emerging Adulthood: The Winding Road From the Late Teens Through the Twenties,* p. 144. New York: Oxford University Press.

391 Interview with the author. Sue Johnson is a pseudonym.

392 Laurence J. Peter, cited in Townsend, Robert (1970), *Up the Organization,* p. 166. New York: Alfred A. Knopf, Inc.

393 Brandon, Emily, "Job Search Grows Cold, Creating Reluctant Retirees," *U.S. News & World Report,* March 3, 2010.

394 Brandon, Emily, "Older Unemployed Remain Out of Work Longer," *U.S. News & World Report,* May 14, 2010.

395 Brandon, Emily, "Older Worker Unemployment Soars Over a Decade," *U.S. News & World Report,* March 5, 2010.

396 Brandon, Emily, "Laid Off Baby Boomers Seek Entry-Level Jobs," *U.S. News & World Report,* July 23, 2009.

397 Ibid.

398 Winerip, Michael, "Time, It Turns Out, Isn't on Their Side," *The New York Times,* March 11, 2010.

399 Brandon, "Job Search Grows Cold, Creating Reluctant Retirees."

400 Dychtwald and Flower, *Age Wave,* p. 174.

401 AARP, 2003. *Staying Ahead of the Curve 2003: The AARP Working in Retirement Study.* Washington, DC, http://www.aarp.org/research/work/employment/.

402 Ryan, *Handbook of U.S. Labor Statistics,* p. 107.

403 Rich, Motoko, "For the Unemployed Over 50, Fears of Never Working Again," *The New York Times,* September 19, 2010.

404 Moeller, Philip, "10 Reasons Seniors Continue to Work," *U.S. News & World Report,* October 7, 2010.

405 Brandon, "Older Worker Unemployment Soars Over a Decade."

406 Townsend, Peter (1963). *The Family Life of Old People.* Baltimore: Penguin Books.

407 Cited in Herbert, Bob, "The Data and the Reality," *The New York Times,* December 27, 2010.

408 Urban Institute and AARP Public Policy Institute, cited in Brandon, Emily, "10 Great Places for Entrepreneurs to Retire," *U.S. News & World Report,* June 29, 2009.

409 Kaufman Foundation, cited in Brandon, "10 Great Places for Entrepreneurs to Retire."

410 Wikipedia entry on "Bill James," http://en.wikipedia.org/wiki/Bill_James#Bibliography.

411 James, Bill (1988). *The Bill James Baseball Abstract 1988,* p. 17. New York: Ballantine Books.

412 Samuelson, "The Mystery of Stubborn Unemployment."

413 Krugman, Paul, "Now and Later," *The New York Times,* June 20, 2010.

414 Newman, Rick, "Why a Rising Unemployment Rate is Good News," *U.S. News & World Report,* May 7, 2010.

415 Zuckerman, "The American Jobs Machine is Clanging to a Halt."

416 Rampell, Catherine, "Unemployed, and Likely to Stay That Way," *The New York Times,* December 2, 2010.

417 Krugman, Paul, "The Forgotten Millions," *The New York Times,* March 17, 2011.

418 Rifkin, *The End of Work,* pp. 239, 290.

419 Herbert, Bob, "A Terrible Divide," *The New York Times,* February 7, 2011.

420 Karabell, "We Are Not in This Together."

421 Owens, Joseph (1976). *Dread: The Rastafarians of Jamaica,* p. 28. Kingston, Jamaica: Sangster.

422 Ibid., p. 30.

423 Ibid., p. 149.

424 Ibid., p. 154.

425 Ibid., pp. 157, 159, 162.

426 Leonard E. Barrett, cited in Owens, *Dread,* p. 23.

427 Gordon, D. and C. Dixon, "La Urbanización en Kingston, Jamaica: Años de Crecimiento y Años de Crisis." In Portes, A. and M. Lungo (eds.), Urbanización en el Caribe FLACSO, San Jose, Costa Rica, pp. 99-211, cited in Clarke, Colin and David Howard, "Contradictory Socio-Economic Consequences of Structural Adjustment in Kingston, Jamaica," *The Geographical Journal,* June 2006.

428 Forrester, Viviane (1996), translated with the assistance of Sheila Malovany-Chevallier, *The Economic Horror,* pp. 51-52. Cambridge, United Kingdom: Polity Press.

429 Choose Milwaukee website, http://www.choosemilwaukee.com/ milwaukee_region_crime_rate.aspx.

430 Neighborhood Scout website, http://www.neighborhoodscout. com/wi/milwaukee/crime/.

431 Wisconsin Manufacturers & Commerce and Milwaukee Journal Sentinel, cited in "Milwaukee, Wisconsin: The Northwest Neighborhood," http://www.frbsf.org/cpreport/docs/milwaukee_ wi.pdf.

432 A. O. Smith Corporation. Source: http://www.aosmith.com/.

433 Kathryn Edin, cited in Peck, "How a New Jobless Era Will Transform America."

434 Wilson, *When Work Disappears,* p. xiii.

435 Ibid., pp. 21, 23. The rates were for Woodlawn and Oakland in 1990.

436 Peck, "How a New Jobless Era Will Transform America."

437 Wilson, *When Work Disappears,* pp. 59-60.

438 Ibid., p. 61.

439 Ibid., pp. 34-35. The companies were Western Electric, International Harvester, and Sears.

440 Ibid., p. 67.

441 Ibid., p. 3.

442 Ibid., p. 64.

443 Peck, "How a New Jobless Era Will Transform America."

444 Foroohar, "Joblessness Is Here to Stay."

445 Meyerson, "Corporate America, Paving a Downward Economic Slide."

446 Steingart, *The War for Wealth,* p. 199.

447 Ibid., p. 200.

448 Bruce Western and Catherine Beckett, cited in Beck, *The Brave New World of Work,* p. 116.

449 Cited in Peck, "How a New Jobless Era Will Transform America."

450 Webber, Alan M., "Reverse Brain Drain Threatens U.S. Economy," *USA Today,* February 23, 2004.

451 Tolson, "A Growing Trend of Leaving America."

452 Cited in Peck, "How a New Jobless Era Will Transform America."

453 Peck, "How a New Jobless Era Will Transform America."

454 Kathryn Edin, cited in Peck, "How a New Jobless Era Will Transform America."

455 Rosin, Hanna, "The End of Men," *The Atlantic,* July/August 2010.

456 W. Bradford Wilcox, cited in Peck, "How a New Jobless Era Will Transform America."

457 Ryan, *Handbook of U.S. Labor Statistics,* p. 10; Bureau of Labor Statistics.

458 Rosin, "The End of Men."

459 Newman, Rick, "How Tough Times Are Helping Women Get Ahead," *U.S. News & World Report,* February 4, 2011.

460 Rosin, "The End of Men."

461 Newman, "How Tough Times Are Helping Women Get Ahead."

462 Rosin, "The End of Men."

463 Peck, "How a New Jobless Era Will Transform America."

464 Till Von Wachter, cited in Peck, "How a New Jobless Era Will Transform America."

465 Krysia Mossakowski, cited in Peck, "How a New Jobless Era Will Transform America."

466 Foroohar, "Joblessness is Here to Stay."

467 Robert P. Putnam, cited in Foroohar, "Joblessness is Here to Stay."

468 Ford, *The Lights in the Tunnel,* pp. 168-169.

469 Peck, "How a New Jobless Era Will Transform America."

Chapter 4: What Do the Papers Say?

470 Zuckerman, "The Great Jobs Recession Goes On."

471 Thompson, Derek, "Hey Obama, Here are 9 Big Ideas to Beat Unemployment," *The Atlantic,* December 2009; Newman, Rick, "What It Will Take for Hiring to Revive," *U.S. News & World Report,* July 2, 2010; McIntyre, Douglas A., Michael B. Sauter, and Ashley C. Allen, "10 Ways to Cut Unemployment in Half," *The Atlantic,* September 2010.

472 Thompson, "Hey Obama, Here are 9 Big Ideas to Beat Unemployment"; McIntyre, Sauter, and Ashley, "10 Ways to Cut Unemployment in Half"; Samuelson, Robert J., "Who's Going to Get the Jobs Machine Going?", *The Washington Post,* October 19, 2009; Mark Thoma, cited in "Can Obama Create More Jobs Soon?", Room For Debate blog, *The New York Times,* June 24, 2010, http://www.nytimes.com/roomfordebate.

473 Thompson, "Hey Obama, Here are 9 Big Ideas to Beat Unemployment"; Newman, "What It Will Take For Hiring to Revive"; McIntyre, Sauter, and Ashley, "10 Ways to Cut Unemployment in Half."

474 Tyler Cowen, cited in "Can Obama Create More Jobs Soon?"

475 Jeffrey A. Miron, cited in "Can Obama Create More Jobs Soon?"

476 Thompson, "Hey Obama, Here are 9 Big Ideas to Beat Unemployment"; Reich, Robert B., "How to End the Great Recession," *The New York Times,* September 2, 2010; Tyler Cowen, cited in "Can Obama Create More Jobs Soon?"

477 Thompson, "Hey Obama, Here are 9 Big Ideas to Beat Unemployment"; McIntyre, Sauter, and Ashley, "10 Ways to Cut Unemployment in Half."

478 Newman, Rick, "3 Ways Obama Could Boost Hiring," *U.S. News & World Report,* September 3, 2010.

479 Reich, "How to End the Great Recession."

480 Jeffrey A. Miron, cited in "Can Obama Create More Jobs Soon?"

481 McIntyre, Sauter, and Ashley, "10 Ways to Cut Unemployment in Half."

482 Cook, Nancy, "Three Big Ideas for Solving Unemployment," Newsweek, July 20, 2010; Reich, "How to End the Great Recession."

483 Heather Boushey, cited in "Can Obama Create More Jobs Soon?"

484 Thompson, "Hey Obama, Here are 9 Big Ideas to Beat Unemployment"; McIntyre, Sauter, and Ashley, "10 Ways to Cut Unemployment in Half."

485 Newman, "What It Will Take For Hiring to Revive"; Newman, "3 Ways Obama Could Boost Hiring"; Samuelson, "Who's Going to Get the Jobs Machine Going?"

486 Heather Boushey, cited in "Can Obama Create More Jobs Soon?"; Mark Thoma, cited in "Can Obama Create More Jobs Soon?"

487 Davis, Steven J., "Getting Back To Work," Forbes, October 2009; Tyler Cowen, cited in "Can Obama Create More Jobs Soon?"; Jeffrey A. Miron, cited in "Can Obama Create More Jobs Soon?"

488 James K. Galbraith, cited in "Can Obama Create More Jobs Soon?"

489 Newman, "What It Will Take for Hiring to Revive."

490 McIntyre, Sauter, and Ashley, "10 Ways to Cut Unemployment in Half."

491 Newman, "3 Ways Obama Could Boost Hiring."

492 Davis, "Getting Back To Work."

493 Jeffrey A. Miron, cited in "Can Obama Create More Jobs Soon?"

Chapter 5: Non-Solutions

494 James Mann, cited in Jacques, Martin (2009), *When China Rules the World: The End of the Western World and the Birth of a New Global Order,* pp. 195-196. New York: The Penguin Press.

495 Foroohar, "Joblessness is Here to Stay."

496 Foroohar, "Where the Jobs Are."

497 Krugman, "Degrees and Dollars."

498 Zuckerman, "Unemployment Rate is Worse Than it Looks."

499 Cited in Gunn, "Betsey Stevenson Answers Your Questions."

500 Wolgemuth, Liz, "Why Everyone Suffers When Job Seekers Give Up," *U.S. News & World Report,* July 14, 2010.

501 Cited in Gunn, "Betsey Stevenson Answers Your Questions."

502 Coppins, McKay, "Georgia's Job Program Works," Newsweek, October 4, 2010.

503 McArdle, "What to Do About Long-Term Unemployment?"

504 Krugman, "Degrees and Dollars."

505 Adler, Ben, "Education Does Not Explain Growth in Inequality," *Newsweek,* December 6, 2010.

506 Friedman, *The World Is Flat,* p. 265.

507 Ibid., p. 25.

508 Krugman, "Degrees and Dollars."

509 Fitzpatrick, Robert L. and Joyce K. Reynolds (1997). *False Profits: Seeking Financial and Spiritual Deliverance in Multi-Level Marketing and Pyramid Schemes,* p. 4. Charlotte, NC: Herald Press.

510 Ibid., p. 10.

511 Ibid., p. 18.

512 Ibid.

513 Paul Klebnikov, cited in Fitzpatrick and Reynolds, *False Profits,* pp. 152-153.

514 Fitzpatrick and Reynolds, *False Profits,* p. 153.

515 Ibid., p. 187.

516 Ibid., p. 130.

517 Ibid., p. 154.

518 Ibid., p. 38.

519 Tyson, Eric, and Jim Schell (2008). *Small Business for Dummies* (3rd ed.), p. 129. Indianapolis, IN: Wiley Publishing, Inc.

520 Adapted from Roberts, Russell (2001), *The Choice: A Fable of Free Trade and Protectionism,* pp. 9-10. Upper Saddle River, NJ: Prentice Hall.

521 Adapted from Harford, Tim (2005), *The Undercover Economist,* p. 194. New York: Random House Trade Paperbacks.

522 David Friedman, cited in Harford, *The Undercover Economist,* p. 198.

523 Harford, *The Undercover Economist,* pp. 195-196.

524 Ibid., pp. 197-198.

525 Ibid., p. 206.

526 Roberts, *The Choice,* p. 10.

527 Harford, *The Undercover Economist,* p. 27.

528 Roberts, *The Choice,* p. 79.

529 Harford, *The Undercover Economist,* p. 193.

530 Roberts, *The Choice,* p. 16.

531 Ibid., pp. 68-69.

532 Harford, *The Undercover Economist,* pp. 190, 211.

533 Roberts, *The Choice,* p. 109.

534 Ibid., p. 84.

535 Yu Yongding, cited in Jacques, *When China Rules the World,* p. 159.

536 Jacques, *When China Rules the World,* p. 159.

537 Zakaria, Fareed (2009). *The Post-American World,* p. 89. New York: W. W. Norton & Company.

538 Angus Maddison, cited in Jacques, *When China Rules the World,* p. 159.

539 Karabell, *Superfusion,* p. 70.

540 Zakaria, *The Post-American World,* p. 91.

541 Karabell, *Superfusion,* p. 32.

542 Yu Yongding, cited in Jacques, *When China Rules the World,* p. 162.

543 Zakaria, *The Post-American World,* p. 89.

544 The Economist, cited in Jacques, *When China Rules the World,* p. 159.

545 Jacques, *When China Rules the World,* p. 189.

546 Karabell, *Superfusion,* p. 223.

547 Clyde Prestowitz, cited in Jacques, *When China Rules the World,* p. 162.

548 Zakaria, *The Post-American World,* p. 91.

549 Jacques, *When China Rules the World,* p. 12.

550 Joseph E. Stiglitz, cited in Jacques, *When China Rules the World,* p. 162.

551 Zakaria, *The Post-American World,* p. 90.

552 Ibid., pp. 99-100.

553 Yu Yongding, cited in Jacques, *When China Rules the World,* p. 189.

554 Robert Scott, cited in Thompson, Derek, "Will Punishing China Really Create Jobs?", *The Atlantic,* October 2010.

555 Karabell, *Superfusion,* p. 303.

556 Freedman, Michael, "The End of the Affair," *Newsweek,* September 24, 2010.

557 *The Wall Street Journal,* cited in Jacques, *When China Rules the World,* p. 189.

558 Jacques, *When China Rules the World,* p. 361.

559 *The Wall Street Journal,* cited in Jacques, *When China Rules the World,* p. 189.

560 "Yuan renminbi" is Mandarin for "people's currency." I hereafter shorten it to "renminbi."

561 Thompson, "Will Punishing China Really Create Jobs?"

562 Zakaria, *The Post-American World,* p. xvii.

563 Robert Scott, cited in Thompson, "Will Punishing China Really Create Jobs?"

564 Freedman, "The End of the Affair."

565 Robert Scott, cited in Thompson, "Will Punishing China Really Create Jobs?"

566 Thompson, "Will Punishing China Really Create Jobs?"

567 Wu, Mark, "China's Currency Isn't Our Problem," *The New York Times,* January 17, 2011.

568 Karabell, *Superfusion,* pp. 137, 313.

569 Zakaria, *The Post-American World,* p. xviii.

570 Jacques, *When China Rules the World,* p. 359.

571 Ibid., p. 360.

572 Steingart, *The War for Wealth,* p. 225.

573 Zakaria, *The Post-American World,* p. 124.

574 Karabell, *Superfusion,* p. 296.

575 Zakaria, *The Post-American World,* p. xx.

576 Cited in Zakaria, *The Post-American World,* p. xx.

577 Karabell, *Superfusion,* p. 296.

578 Jacques, *When China Rules the World,* p. 360.

579 Karabell, *Superfusion,* p. 279.

580 Ibid., p. 291.

581 Jacques, *When China Rules the World,* p. 12.

582 Ibid., pp. 13, 197.

583 Suisheng Zhao, cited in Jacques, *When China Rules the World,* pp. 240-241.

584 Jacques, *When China Rules the World,* p. 241.

585 Ibid., p. 244.

586 Robert Scott, cited in Thompson, "Will Punishing China Really Create Jobs?"

587 Ford, *The Lights in the Tunnel,* p. 123.

588 Dominic Wilson and Anna Stupnytska, cited in Jacques, *When China Rules the World,* p. 3.

589 Karabell, *Superfusion,* p. 288.

590 Ford, *The Lights in the Tunnel,* p. 119.

591 Jacques, *When China Rules the World,* p. 164.

592 Ford, *The Lights in the Tunnel,* pp. 118, 123.

593 Jacques, *When China Rules the World,* p. 427.

594 Zakaria, *The Post-American World,* p. 102.

595 Ford, *The Lights in the Tunnel,* pp. 118-119.

596 Yu Yongding, cited in Jacques, *When China Rules the World,* p. 163.

597 Jacques, *When China Rules the World,* pp. 165, 363.

598 Friedman, *The Next 100 Years,* pp. 95, 96, 98.

599 Lester R. Brown, cited in Jacques, *When China Rules the World,* p. 169.

600 Jacques, *When China Rules the World,* p. 363.

601 Friedman, *The Next 100 Years,* pp. 88, 96, 97.

602 Zakaria, *The Post-American World,* pp. 98-99.

603 Karabell, *Superfusion,* p. 12.

Chapter 6: Partial Solutions

604 Tyson and Schell, *Small Business for Dummies,* p. 1.

605 Jeffrey S. Passel and Robert Suro, cited in Chomsky, Aviva (2007), *They Take Our Jobs!": And 20 Other Myths About Immigration,* p. xiv. Boston: Beacon Press

606 Chomsky, *They Take Our Jobs!,* p. 59.

607 Jeffrey S. Passel, cited in Chomsky, *They Take Our Jobs!,* p. 59.

608 Riley, Jason L. (2008). *Let Them In: The Case for Open Borders,* p. 57. New York: Gotham Books.

609 Geoge J. Borjas and Lawrence F. Katz, cited in Mishel, Bernstein, and Shierholz, *The State of Working America 2008/2009,* p. 197.

610 Meissner, Doris, "5 Myths About Immigration," *The Washington Post,* May 2, 2010; Riley, *Let Them In,* p. 57.

611 Chomsky, *They Take Our Jobs!*, p. 16.

612 Ibid., p. 167.

613 Ibid., p. 44.

614 Riley, *Let Them In,* p. 119.

615 Chomsky, *They Take Our Jobs!*, pp. 37-38.

616 Eduardo Porter, cited in Chomsky, *They Take Our Jobs!*, p. 38.

617 Riley, *Let Them In,* p. 68.

618 Bureau of Labor Statistics, cited in Riley, *Let Them In,* p. 70.

619 Mishel, Bernstein, and Shierholz, *The State of Working America 2008/2009,* p. 163.

620 Ibid., p. 168.

621 Riley, *Let Them In,* p. 59.

622 Chomsky, *They Take Our Jobs!*, p. 37.

623 James P. Smith and Barry Edmonston, cited in Krikorian, Mark (2008), *The New Case Against Immigration: Both Legal and Illegal,* p. 138. New York: Sentinel.

624 Riley, *Let Them In,* p. 57.

625 Andrew Sum, Paul Harrington, and Ishwar Khatiwada, cited in Krikorian, *The New Case Against Immigration,* pp. 142-143.

626 Pew Hispanic Center, cited in Herbert, "Hiding from Reality."

627 Krikorian, *The New Case Against Immigration,* p. 133.

628 James P. Smith and Barry Edmonston, cited in Krikorian, *The New Case Against Immigration,* p. 139.

629 Meissner, "5 Myths About Immigration."

630 George J. Borjas, cited in Krikorian, *The New Case Against Immigration,* p. 139.

631 Giovanni Peri, cited in Riley, *Let Them In,* p. 59.

632 Thomas Muller, cited in Riley, *Let Them In,* p. 61.

633 Nolan Malone, Kaali Baluja, Joseph M. Costanzo, and Cynthia J. Davis, cited in Chomsky, *They Take Our Jobs!*, p. 8.

634 Chomsky, *They Take Our Jobs!*, p. 8.

635 Riley, *Let Them In,* p. 73.

636 Ibid., p. 75.

637 Chomsky, *They Take Our Jobs!*, p. 16.

638 Cable News Network, cited in Chomsky, *They Take Our Jobs!*, p. 16.

639 Meissner, "5 Myths About Immigration."

640 Riley, *Let Them In,* p. 71.

641 Ibid., p. 74.

642 Ibid., p. 72.

643 Cited in Riley, *Let Them In,* p. 63.

644 Zuckerman, "The American Jobs Machine is Clanging to a Halt."

645 Cited in Zuckerman, "The American Jobs Machine is Clanging to a Halt."

646 Cited in Riley, *Let Them In,* p. 74.

647 Krikorian, *The New Case Against Immigration,* pp. 133, 149, 150, 156.

648 George J. Borjas, cited in Krikorian, *The New Case Against Immigration,* p. 161.

649 Krikorian, *The New Case Against Immigration,* pp. 160-161; Ford, *The Lights in the Tunnel,* pp. 90-91.

650 Krugman, "Degrees and Dollars."

651 Wolgemuth, Liz, "Why Start-Ups Could Make or Break the Job Recovery," *U.S. News & World Report,* July 19, 2010.

652 John C. Haltiwanger, Ron S. Jarmin, and Javier Miranda, cited in Indiviglio, Daniel, "Young, Not Small, Businesses Drive Job Growth," *The Atlantic,* September 2010.

653 Tyson and Schell, *Small Business for Dummies,* p. 101.

654 Ibid., p. 42.

655 Nemko, Marty, "Overrated Career: Small Business Owner," *U.S. News & World Report,* December 11, 2008.

656 Tyson and Schell, *Small Business for Dummies,* p. 48.

657 Nemko, "Overrated Career."

658 Tyson and Schell, *Small Business for Dummies,* pp. 18-21.

659 Warner, Ralph, and Laurence, Bethany (2009). *Save Your Small Business: 10 Crucial Strategies to Survive Hard Times or Close Down and Move On,* p. 6. Berkeley, CA: Nolo.

660 Tyson and Schell, *Small Business for Dummies,* pp. 22-23.

661 Ibid., pp. 24-25.

662 Ibid., pp. 31, 34.

663 Nemko, "Overrated Career."

664 Samuelson, Robert J., "The Real Jobs Machine: Entrepreneurs," *The Washington Post,* October 4, 2010.

665 Thompson, Derek, "Actually, America Isn't a Small Business Country At All," *The Atlantic,* August 2009.

666 Newman, Rick, "Why Startups Surged During the Recession," *U.S. News & World Report,* May 20, 2010.

667 Warner and Laurence, *Save Your Small Business,* p. 4.

668 Newman, "Why Startups Surged During the Recession."

669 Ledbetter, James, "Death of a Salesman. Of Lots of Them, Actually," *Slate* blog, September 21, 2010, http://www.slate.com/.

670 Goodman, "The New Poor."

671 Ledbetter, "Death of a Salesman. Of Lots of Them, Actually."

672 Ziglar, Zig (2003). *Selling 101,* p. 4. Nashville, TN: Thomas Nelson, Inc.

673 Ibid., p. 1.

674 Lytle, Chris (2000). *The Accidental Salesperson: How to Take Control of Your Sales Career and Earn the Respect and Income You Deserve,* p. 21. New York: Amacom

675 Ziglar, *Selling 101,* p. 17.

676 Lytle, *The Accidental Salesperson,* p. 11.

677 Ziglar, *Selling 101,* p. 3.

678 Sloan, Allan, Newmyer, Tory, and Burke, Doris, "In This Recovery, Washington Has Less Power Over the Economy Than You Think," *The Washington Post,* October 17, 2010.

679 Thompson, "CBO Counters Liberals."

680 Newman, "Why Politicians Can't Create Real Jobs."

681 Samuelson, Robert J., "The Economic Blame Game," Newsweek, September 18, 2010.

682 Romano, Andrew, "Estimates Say Fewer Jobs, Larger Deficits if Republicans Were in Charge," *Newsweek,* August 27, 2010.

683 Gross, Daniel, "Are You Feeling Stimulated Yet?", *Newsweek,* February 17, 2010.

684 Harwood, "Mystery for White House."

685 "New White House Report Claims More Jobs From Stimulus Bill," *U.S. News & World Report,* July 14, 2010.

686 Romano, "Estimates Say Fewer Jobs, Larger Deficits if Republicans Were in Charge."

687 "The September Report," *The New York Times,* October 8, 2010.

688 Samuelson, Robert J., "Judging Obama's Economics," *The Washington Post,* January 3, 2011.

689 Sloan, Newmyer, and Burke, "In This Recovery, Washington Has Less Power Over the Economy Than You Think."

690 Zakaria, Fareed, "A Lonely Success," *Newsweek,* September 19, 2010.

691 Ibid.

692 Sloan, Newmyer, and Burke, "In This Recovery, Washington Has Less Power over the Economy Than You Think."

Chapter 7: Valuable Possibilities

693 Cutler, *Your Money or Your Life,* p. 120.

694 Bazinet, Kenneth R., "Obama to Roll Out $50 Billion Jobs Proposal," *U.S. News & World Report,* September 8, 2010.

695 Klein, Ezra, "If You Build It…", *Newsweek,* October 2, 2010.

696 Thompson, "Will Punishing China Really Create Jobs?"

697 Rampell, "Unemployed, and Likely to Stay That Way."

698 Thompson, "Will Punishing China Really Create Jobs?"; Herbert, Bob, "The Magic Potion."

699 Klein, "If You Build It…"

700 Aronowitz, Stanley, Dawn Esposito, William DiFazio, and Margaret Yard, "The Post-Work Manifesto." In Aronowitz, Stanley and Cutler, Jonathan (eds.) (1998), *Post-Work: The Wages of Cybernation,* p. 33. New York: Routledge.

701 Wilson, *When Work Disappears,* pp. 237-238.

702 Felix Rohatyn, cited in Rifkin, The End of Work, p. 264.

703 Klein, "If You Build It…"

704 Rampell, "Unemployed, and Likely to Stay That Way."

705 Adler, "Education Does Not Explain Growth in Inequality."

706 The Washington Post, *Landmark,* pp. 101, 153.

707 Herzlinger, Regina, "Why Republicans Should Back Universal Health Care," *The Atlantic,* April 2009.

708 Thompson, "Actually, America Isn't a Small Business Country at All."

709 Rob Fairlie, cited in Shane, Scott A., "How the Health Care Mess Affects Entrepreneurship," Economix blog, *The New York Times,* July 27, 2009, http://economix.blogs.nytimes.com/.

710 Shane, "How the Health Care Mess Affects Entrepreneurship."

711 Herzlinger, "Why Republicans Should Back Universal Health Care."

712 The Washington Post, *Landmark,* p. 159.

713 *The Wall Street Journal,* cited in Mahar, *Money-Driven Medicine,* pp. xiv-xv.

714 Lawrence H. Summers, cited in Eibner, *The Economic Burden of Providing Health Insurance,* p. 3.

715 Kanika Kapur, cited in Eibner, *The Economic Burden of Providing Health Insurance,* p. 3.

716 Shapiro, *What Does Somebody Have to Do to Get a Job Around Here?,* pp. 13-14.

717 David M. Cutler and Brigitte C. Madrian, cited in Eibner, *The Economic Burden of Providing Health Insurance,* p. 3.

718 Cutler, *Your Money or Your Life,* pp. 119-120.

719 *The Washington Post, Landmark,* p. 81.

720 *CIA World Factbook,* cited in Cohen, "Boehner's Health Delusion."

721 T. R. Reid, cited in Cohen, "Boehner's Health Delusion."

722 Cohen, "Boehner's Health Delusion."

723 Karen Donelan et al., cited in Cutler, *Your Money or Your Life,* p. ix.

724 Cohen, "Boehner's Health Delusion."

725 G. Anderson and P. S. Hussey, cited in Bodenheimer and Grumbach, *Understanding Health Policy,* p. 173.

726 Organization for Economic Cooperation and Development, cited in Mishel, Bernstein, and Shierholz, *The State of Working America 2008/2009,* p. 351.

727 Mahar, *Money-Driven Medicine,* p. 2.

728 Bodenheimer and Grumbach, *Understanding Health Policy,* pp. 163, 166.

729 G. Anderson and P. S. Hussey, cited in Bodenheimer and Grumbach, *Understanding Health Policy,* p. 173.

730 See Bodenheimer and Grumbach, *Understanding Health Policy,* pp. 160-173.

731 David M. Cutler and Brigitte C. Madrian, cited in Eibner, *The Economic Burden of Providing Health Insurance,* p. 2.

732 Surowiecki, James, "The Fifth Wheel," *The New Yorker,* January 4, 2010.

733 Reid, T. R., "Five Myths About Health Care in the World," *The Washington Post,* August 23, 2009.

734 Ford, *The Lights in the Tunnel,* p. 187.

735 Cited in Goodman, "The New Poor."

736 Kaufman, *Professionals in Search of Work,* p. 246; Thompson, Derek, "The Case For and Against Unemployment Insurance," *The Atlantic,* July 2010.

737 Thompson, Derek, "This Is What an Unemployment Crisis Looks Like," *The Atlantic,* June 2010.

738 Gross, Daniel, "Does Anyone Care About Unemployment Anymore?", *Newsweek,* July 1, 2010.

739 Cited in Thompson, "The Case For and Against Unemployment Insurance."

740 "February's Jobs Report."

741 Rosen, Nick (2010). *Off the Grid: Inside the Movement for More Space, Less Government, and True Independence in Modern America,* p. 13. New York: Penguin Books.

742 Ibid., pp. 5, 14, 15.

743 Ibid., p. 6.

744 Rosen, *Off the Grid,* pp. 97-98; Freed, Dolly (1978, reprinted 2010). *Possum Living: How to Live Well Without a Job and With (Almost) No Money,* pp. 13, 164, 166, 171. Portland, OR: Tin House Books.

745 Freed, *Possum Living,* pp. 13, 34.

746 Rosen, *Off the Grid,* pp. 131, 132, 135.

747 Ibid., pp. 219, 237.

748 Ibid., p. 281.

749 Freed, *Possum Living,* pp. 15-16.

750 Rosen, *Off the Grid,* p. 133.

751 Freed, *Possum Living,* p. 152.

752 Rosen, *Off the Grid,* pp. 97, 187.

753 Freed, *Possum Living,* p. 148.

754 Rosen, *Off the Grid,* p. 130.

755 Freed, *Possum Living,* p. 27.

756 Ibid., p. 173.

757 Ibid., pp. 193-201.

758 Rosen, *Off the Grid,* p. 5.

759 Ibid., p. 11.

760 Ibid., p. 186.

761 Freed, *Possum Living,* p. 9.

762 Rosen, *Off the Grid*, p. 97.

763 Freed, *Possum Living*, p. 185.

764 Clyatt, Bob (2007). *Work Less, Live More: The Way to Semi-Retirement* (2nd ed.). Berkeley, CA: Nolo.

765 Fisker, Jacob Lund (2010). *Early Retirement Extreme: A Philosophical and Practical Guide to Financial Independence.* USA: softcover book published by www.earlyretirementextreme.com

766 Clyatt, *Work Less, Live More*, p. 4.

767 Fisker, *Early Retirement Extreme*, p. 4.

768 Ibid., p. 85.

769 Ibid., pp. 127, 128, 132.

770 Clyatt, *Work Less, Live More*, p. 145.

771 Fisker, *Early Retirement Extreme*, pp. 135, 176, 177.

772 Clyatt, *Work Less, Live More*, pp. 15-16.

773 Ibid., p. 78.

774 Ibid., p. 81.

775 Fisker, *Early Retirement Extreme*, p. 40.

776 Clyatt, *Work Less, Live More*, p. 152.

777 Ibid., p. 18.

778 Ibid., p. 148.

779 Ibid., pp. 272, 273, 275, 289.

780 Fisker, *Early Retirement Extreme*, p. 41.

781 Clyatt, *Work Less, Live More*, pp. 312-313.

782 Samuelson, Robert J., "Our Giveaway Farm Programs," *Newsweek,* September 15, 2007.

783 Gibney, James, "Tell Americans What They're Really Paying for Their Food," *The Atlantic,* July 2009.

784 Samuelson, "Our Giveaway Farm Programs."

785 Imhoff, Daniel (2006), *Food Fight: The Citizen's Guide to a Food and Farm Bill,* p. 19. Healdsburg, CA: Watershed Media.

786 Ibid., pp. 22, 25.

787 Camahan, Ira, "Milking the Farm Program," *Forbes,* July 21, 2004.

788 Imhoff, *Food Fight,* p. 59.

789 Daniel Sumner, cited in Dubner, Stephen J., "The Illogic of Farm Subsidies, and Other Agricultural Truths," Freakonomics blog, July 24, 2008, http://www.freakonomics.com/blog/.

790 Samuelson, "Our Giveaway Farm Programs."

791 Thurow, Roger and Kilman, Scott (2009). *Enough: Why the World's Poorest Starve in an Age of Plenty,* p. 57. New York: Public Affairs.

792 Imhoff, *Food Fight,* p. 16.

793 *The New York Times,* January 15, 2011.

794 Gibney, "Tell Americans What They're Really Paying for Their Food."

795 Samuelson, "Our Giveaway Farm Programs."

796 United States Department of Agriculture Economic Research Service, cited in Imhoff, *Food Fight,* p. 40.

797 Samuelson, "Our Giveaway Farm Programs."

798 Imhoff, *Food Fight,* p. 39.

799 Peter Riggs, cited in Imhoff, *Food Fight,* pp. 39-42.

800 Heritage Foundation, cited in Camahan, "Milking the Farm Program."

801 Camahan, "Milking the Farm Program."

802 Gibney, "Tell Americans What They're Really Paying for Their Food."

803 Camahan, "Milking the Farm Program."

804 Imhoff, *Food Fight,* p. 22.

805 Ibid., p. 53.

806 Daniel Sumner, cited in Dubner, "The Illogic of Farm Subsidies, and Other Agricultural Truths."

807 U.S. International Trade Commission, cited in Gibney, "Tell Americans What They're Really Paying for Their Food."

808 Daniel Sumner, cited in Dubner, "The Illogic of Farm Subsidies, and Other Agricultural Truths."

809 Samuelson, "Our Giveaway Farm Programs."

810 Imhoff, *Food Fight,* p. 19.

811 Thurow and Kilman, *Enough: Why the World's Poorest Starve in an Age of Plenty,* p. xvii.

812 See Imhoff, *Food Fight,* pp. 90-97.

813 *Newsweek,* January 15, 2011.

814 Karabell, *Superfusion,* pp. 222-223.

815 Quigley, William P. (2003). *Ending Poverty as We Know It: Guaranteeing a Right to a Job at a Living Wage,* p. 142. Philadelphia: Temple University Press.

816 Gross, "Does Anyone Care About Unemployment Anymore?"

817 Newman, "Why Politicians Can't Create Real Jobs."

818 Walsh, Kenneth T., "Obama's Job No. 1: Create Jobs, Strengthen the Economy," *U.S. News & World Report*, January 28, 2010.

819 Samuelson, "The Economic Blame Game."

820 Quigley, *Ending Poverty as We Know It*, p. 141.

821 Cited in Quigley, *Ending Poverty as We Know It*, pp. 142-143.

822 Ford, *The Lights in the Tunnel*, pp. 142-143.

823 McArdle, "What to Do About Long-Term Unemployment?"

824 Gross, "Does Anyone Care About Unemployment Anymore?"

825 "Minimum Wage History," http://oregonstate.edu/instruct/anth484/minwage.html.

826 Filion, Kai, "Tables, figures, and data download—Minimum Wage Issue Guide," Economic Policy Institute, http://www.epi.org/publications/entry/tables_figures_data/.

827 Quigley, *Ending Poverty as We Know It*, p. 134.

828 Cited in Quigley, *Ending Poverty as We Know It*, p. 134.

829 Evans, Christopher (1979). *The Micro Millennium*, p. 151. New York: The Viking Press.

830 Rifkin, *The End of Work*, p. xxvii.

831 Gans, Herbert J., "Foreword." In Best, Fred (1988), *Reducing Workweeks to Prevent Layoffs*, p. xix. Philadelphia: Temple University Press.

832 Ibid.

833 Aronowitz et al., "The Post-Work Manifesto," in Aronowitz and Cutler, *Post-Work*, p. 59.

834 Williams, Colin C. (2007). *Rethinking the Future of Work: Directions and Visions*, p. 120. Basingstoke, United Kingdom: Palgrave Macmillan.

835 Cited in Gunn, "Betsey Stevenson Answers Your Questions."

836 Evans, *The Micro Millennium*, p. 151.

837 Gans, "Foreword," in Best, *Reducing Workweeks to Prevent Layoffs*, p. xix.

838 Aronowitz et al., "The Post-Work Manifesto," in Aronowitz and Cutler, *Post-Work*, p. 61.

839 Rifkin, *The End of Work*, pp. xxviii-xxx.

840 Ford, *The Lights in the Tunnel*, pp. 185-186.

841 Cited in Gunn, "Betsey Stevenson Answers Your Questions."

842 Best, *Reducing Workweeks to Prevent Layoffs,* p. 3.

843 Pearlstein, "Wage Cuts Hurt, But They May Be the Only Way to Get Americans Back to Work."

844 Best, *Reducing Workweeks to Prevent Layoffs,* p. 19.

845 See O'Hanlon, Mary and Morella, Angela (2003), *Job Sharing,* pp. 2-3. Crows Nest, Australia: Allen & Unwin.

846 Best, *Reducing Workweeks to Prevent Layoffs,* pp. 3, 262.

847 Cited in Gunn, "Betsey Stevenson Answers Your Questions"; O'Hanlon and Morella, *Job Sharing,* p. 7.

848 O'Hanlon and Morella, *Job Sharing,* pp. 5, 6, 11.

849 Cited in Gunn, "Betsey Stevenson Answers Your Questions."

850 Aronowitz et al., "The Post-Work Manifesto," in Aronowitz and Cutler, *Post-Work,* p. 76.

Chapter 8: Thinking the Not-So-Unthinkable: Guaranteed Income

851 Aronowitz et al., "The Post-Work Manifesto," in Aronowitz and Cutler, *Post-Work,* p. 65.

852 Ford, "What If There's No Fix for High Unemployment?"

853 Rifkin, *The End of Work,* p. 257.

854 Ibid., p. 258.

855 Ibid., p. 259.

856 Ibid., p. 258.

857 Ibid., p. 259.

858 Ibid., pp. 262-263.

859 Williams, *Rethinking the Future of Work,* p. 236.

860 Ibid., p. 235.

861 Beck, *The Brave New World of Work,* p. 126.

862 Guy Standing, cited in Wallulis, *The New Insecurity,* p. 185.

863 Ford, *The Lights in the Tunnel,* p. 172.

864 Ibid., pp. 173-177.

865 Ibid., p. 178.

866 Quigley, *Ending Poverty as We Know It,* p. 3.

867 Ibid., pp. 4, 13.

868 Ibid., pp. 3, 16.

869 Kathryn H. Porter and Allen Dupree, cited in Quigley, *Ending Poverty as We Know It,* p. 5.

870 Williams, *Rethinking the Future of Work,* p. 234.

871 See Williams, *Rethinking the Future of Work,* p. 233.

872 Cited in Chancer, Lynn, "Benefitting from Pragmatic Vision, Part I: The Case for Guaranteed Income in Principle," in Aronowitz and Cutler, *Post-Work,* p. 83.

873 Cited in Rifkin, *The End of Work,* p. 261.

874 Chancer, "Benefitting from Pragmatic Vision, Part II," in Aronowitz and Cutler, *Post-Work,* pp. 85-86.

875 Cited in Rifkin, *The End of Work,* p. 261.

876 Derek Hum and Wayne Simpson, cited in Rifkin, *The End of Work,* p. 262.

877 Rifkin, *The End of Work,* p. 262.

878 Herrnstein, Richard J. and Murray, Charles (1994). *The Bell Curve: Intelligence and Class Structure in American Life,* p. 547. New York: The Free Press.

879 Ford, *The Lights in the Tunnel,* pp. 201-204.

880 Ibid., p. 160.

881 Ibid., p. 180.

882 Ibid., p. 188.

883 Krikorian, *The New Case Against Immigration,* p. 134.

884 Zuckerman, "The American Jobs Machine is Clanging to a Halt."

885 Kahn, Herman, William Brown, and Leon Martel (1976). *The Next 200 Years: A Scenario for America and the World,* pp. 22, 23, 53. New York: William Morrow and Company, Inc.

886 Friedman, *The World Is Flat,* p. 270.

887 U.S. Department of Commerce and U.S. Department of Labor, cited in Kahn, Brown, and Martel, *The Next 200 Years,* p. 52.

888 Krikorian, *The New Case Against Immigration,* p. 2.

889 U.S. Department of Commerce and U.S. Department of Labor, cited in Kahn, Brown, and Martel, *The Next 200 Years,* p. 52.

890 Krugman, "Degrees and Dollars."

891 U.S. Department of Commerce and U.S. Department of Labor, cited in Kahn, Brown, and Martel, *The Next 200 Years,* p. 52.

892 Calculated from Ryan, *Handbook of U.S. Labor Statistics,* p. 9, and Bureau of Labor Statistics.

893 Helen Lachs Ginsburg et al., cited in Quigley, *Ending Poverty as We Know It,* p. 155.

894 Herrnstein and Murray, *The Bell Curve,* p. 547.

895 Aronowitz et al., "The Post-Work Manifesto," in Aronowitz and Cutler, *Post-Work,* p. 67.

896 Chancer, "Benefitting from Pragmatic Vision, Part II," in Aronowitz and Cutler, *Post-Work,* p. 112.

897 Aronowitz et al., "The Post-Work Manifesto," in Aronowitz and Cutler, *Post-Work,* p. 67.

898 Cited in Beck, *The Brave New World of Work,* pp. 111-112.

899 Vonnegut, *Player Piano.*

900 Kahn, Brown, and Martel, *The Next 200 Years,* p. 196.

901 Ibid., p. 203.

902 Rifkin, *The End of Work,* p. 13.

Chapter 9: How Can We Adjust? Changing Our Lives and Our Heads

903 The Quote Garden website, www.quotegarden.com/change.html.

904 Cauchon, Dennis, "Our Standard of Living: Is it Better Than Ever?", *USA Today,* February 3, 2011.

905 Newman, Rick, "Why You Might Be Better Off Than You Think," *U.S. News & World Report,* January 20, 2011.

906 Cauchon, "Our Standard of Living."

907 Newman, "Why You Might Be Better Off Than You Think."

908 Cauchon, "Our Standard of Living."

909 Samuelson, Robert J., "Defining Poverty Up," *Newsweek,* May 30, 2010.

910 Quigley, *Ending Poverty as We Know It,* p. 39.

911 Newman, "New Rules for a Darwinian Economy."

912 Palmer, Kimberly, "A Financial Roadmap for Generation Y," *U.S. News & World Report,* July 21, 2009.

913 Samuelson, Robert J, "Remodeling the American Dream," *Newsweek,* August 23, 2010.

914 Baird, Julia, "Redefining Failure," Newsweek, September 12, 2010.

915 Rifkin, *The End of Work,* p. 216.

916 Beck, *The Brave New World of Work,* p. 10.

917 Gorz, *Reclaiming Work,* p. 1.

918 Williams, *Rethinking the Future of Work,* p. 220.

919 Gallup Monthly, cited in Gorz, *Reclaiming Work*, p. 63.

920 Rifkin, *The End of Work*, p. xxiii.

921 Ibid., p. 293.

922 Gorz, *Reclaiming Work*, p. 3.

923 Aronowitz et al., "The Post-Work Manifesto," in Aronowitz and Cutler, *Post-Work*, p. 71.

924 Beck, *The Brave New World of Work*, pp. 125, 127.

925 Baird, "Redefining Failure."

926 J. Q. Wilson, cited in Herrnstein and Murray, *The Bell Curve*, p. 539.

927 D. T. Ellwood, cited in Herrnstein and Murray, *The Bell Curve*, p. 539.

928 Putnam, Robert D. (2000). *Bowling Alone: The Collapse and Revival of American Community*, p. 288. New York: Simon & Schuster Paperbacks.

929 Herrnstein and Murray, *The Bell Curve*, p. 539.

930 Ibid., p. 540.

931 Rifkin, *The End of Work*, pp. 244-245.

932 Herrnstein and Murray, *The Bell Curve*, p. 540.

933 Rifkin, *The End of Work*, pp. 217, 292.

934 Peck, "How a New Jobless Era Will Transform America."

935 Rifkin, *The End of Work*, p. 239.

936 Virginia A. Hodgkinson and Murray S. Weitzman, cited in Rifkin, *The End of Work*, p. 241.

937 Nonprofit Almanac 1992–1993: Dimensions of the Independent Sector, cited in Rifkin, *The End of Work*, p. 241.

938 Virginia A. Hodgkinson and Murray S. Weitzman, cited in Rifkin, *The End of Work*, p. 242.

939 Rifkin, *The End of Work*, p. 255.

940 Putnam, B*owling Alone*, pp. 296, 297, 300.

941 Ibid., p. 309.

942 Ibid., pp. 309, 330.

943 Ibid., p. 319.

944 Ibid., p. 289.

945 Lisa Berkman, cited in Putnam, *Bowling Alone*, p. 327.

946 Putnam, *Bowling Alone*, p. 289.

947 Ibid., p. 326.

948 Rifkin, *The End of Work,* pp. xxxvii-xxxviii.

949 Rosen, *Off the Grid*, p. 174.

950 Ibid., p. 179.

951 E. Cahn, cited in Williams, *Rethinking the Future of Work*, p. 258.

952 P. Glover, cited in Williams, *Rethinking the Future of Work,* p. 259.

953 Elderplan, cited in Rifkin, *The End of Work,* p. xxxix.

954 E. Collom, cited in Williams, *Rethinking the Future of Work,* p. 259.

955 Rifkin, *The End of Work,* p. xxxviii.

956 Ibid., p. xl.

Postscript: Back to Us

957 The Quote Garden website, www.quotegarden.com/change.html.

958 Cited in Arnett, *Adolescence and Emerging Adulthood,* p. 353.

959 Rifkin, *The End of Work,* pp. 291, 293.

960 Cited in Beck, *The Brave New World of Work,* p. 114.

961 Beck, *The Brave New World of Work,* p. 43.

962 Ford, *The Lights in the Tunnel,* p. 5.

963 Steingart, *The War for Wealth,* p. 17.

964 Ibid., p. 8.

965 Baird, "Redefining Failure."

966 Peck, "How a New Jobless Era Will Transform America."

967 Brainy Quote website, http://www.brainyquote.com/.

Index

Page numbers followed by *f* indicate figures

AARP, 68, 87
Ad Hoc Committee on the
    Triple Revolution, 43, 77
adjusting expectations
    attitudes toward work,
        154–155
    lifestyles, 153–154
    revaluing communities,
        155–157
adulthood *See* full adulthood
advertising for jobs, 71–73
Afghanistan, 73
age
    adult career span, 80
    of employed immigrants,
        118
    employment opportunities
        and, 82–84
    full adulthood, 80–85
    retirement, 66–69, 80,
        87–89
    unemployment and, 23–27,
        28, 31, 86–87, 94
"Age of Austerity," 39
Agricultural Adjustment Act,
    135
agriculture, 119, 136–137, 148

algorithmic skills, 49
Allen, Ashley C., 99
alternative types of employment,
    134–135
The American dream, 40–41
American Enterprise Institute,
    145
American expatriates, 31,
    35–36, 96
American Recovery and
    Reinvestment Act, 125
American Society of Civil
    Engineers, 127
AmeriCorps, 144, 146
Amway, 106, 107
A.O. Smith (business), 92–93
Arendt, Hannah, 77
Arnett, Jeffrey, 80, 85
Aronowitz, Stanley, 143
Ashland City (Tennessee), 93
Association of Americans
    Resident Overseas, 31
AT&T, 48, 50, 56
attending school/training, 30,
    35
Austin (Texas), 157
Australia/Australians, 123, 130,
    141

automatability, 56–57
automation
    in China, 114
    discussion, 43–44, 52, 104
    effects on employment, 45–48,
        51–52, 76, 124, 140
    limits to, 48–51
    scalability and, 56–57
automobile industry, 45, 93

baby boomers, 66–69, 79–80, 87,
    89
Baird, Julia, 154, 155, 160
Bangladesh, 73
Bartik, Timothy, 138
Baseball Abstract 1988, 89
Baylor University Hospital, 58
Beck, Ulrich, 154, 159
benefits
    employer paid, 65–66, 93
    health insurance, 58–61, 63,
        128–130
    unemployment insurance,
        100, 128, 132, 141
Bernanke, Ben, 38, 121
Bernstein, Jared, 139
birth control, 82
Blinder, Alan, 75, 125
Blitz, Steven, 21
Blue Cross/Blue Shield, 58
Bolles, Richard, 29
Borjas, George, 119
Boushey, Heather, 99
Bowling Alone, 98
Brazil, 74, 111
Brooklyn, New York, 157–158
Brown, Lester R., 115
Bush-era tax cuts, 100
business sales, 56, 76

California, 118, 119
Canada/Canadians, 108, 123,
    130, 131, 141
casino gambling, 55–56
Caterpillar, 136

Center for Immigration Studies,
    120
Cerami, Charles, 138
Chapman, Jeff, 139
charitable/non-profit
    organizations, 143, 144, 156
Chevron Texaco, 136
Chicago (Illinois), 32, 93, 94
"Chimerica," 112
China/Chinese
    conforming to Western values,
        103
    currency value, 112, 113–114
    economic and political future,
        114–116
    economic policies, 100, 102
    economic progress, 110–111
    exports, 21
    globalization and, 21, 22, 73,
        74, 113
    immigrants to America, 40
    jobs with American
        companies, 21, 74, 93
    trade with America, 110–117,
        138
Chrysler Corporation, 129
citizen's income, 145
clerical jobs, 44–45
Clinton, Bill, 69
Clyatt, Bob, 133, 134
Commission on Automation,
    Technology, and Economic
    Progress, 44
commodity subsidies, 135–136
comparative advantage, 107–110
competition and globalization, 74
computers, 43–45, 48–49, 50–51
constitutional amendment for
    guaranteed jobs, 144–145
Consumer Price Index, 138
consumers and consumption, 56,
    57, 74, 112, 114, 132, 137,
    138, 142, 147, 153
Cook, Nancy, 99
corn, 135–136

corporate profitability *vs.* employment levels, 38–40
Costa Rica, 134
costs
  governmental farm subsidies, 135–138
  health care and insurance, 59–61, 129–131
cotton, 136
Cowen, Tyler, 18, 99
currency, value of, 75–76, 112, 113–114
Cutler, David M., 127
Cypress Semiconductors, 120

Davis, Steven J., 99
Death of a Salesman (Miller), 154
delayed adulthood, 82
Deng Xiaoping, 73
Detroit (Michigan), 34
DeWine, Mike, Sen., 137
DiFazio, William, 143
Dillo Trading Club, 157
Diogenes, 133
direct federal payments to states, 100
disabilities and ill health, 30, 35
discouraged workers, 30, 34
dollar, value of, 75–76
Dominican Republic, 134
Dooley, Cal, Rep., 137
downsizing, 76
drug use, 92, 93–94
Dubai, 65
"dumping," 109

Earned Income Credit, 145, 146
eBay, 47, 105
economic activity, 105–107
economic factors and employment status, 27–29
economic limitations, 147
Economic Policy Institute, 71, 112, 139
economic stimulus money, 125–126

The Economist, 150
Ecuador, 134
education
  employment status and, 28–29, 30
  increasing/tailoring for employment, 103–105
  levels of, 74, 82–83, 97, 117–118
  wages and, 118–119
efficiency, 45, 48, 62, 120, 134
Einstein, Albert, 160
Eisenhower, Dwight D., 159
Elderplan HMO, 158
"emerging adulthood," 80, 85
Employee Free Choice Act, 101
employees
  excess capacity of, 34, 76, 77, 104
  health plans, 58–61, 63, 128–131, 142
  older age of, 67, 68–69
  paid benefits, 65–66, 93
  reduction of benefits, 63
  retraining, 100, 103–105
  self-employed, 89, 123, 124, 128
  supply and demand for, 63–64
employee sickness funds, 58
employers
  employer-based health insurance, 58–61, 63, 128–130, 142
  paid benefits for employees, 65–66, 93
employment
  alternative types of, 134–135
  automation effects on, 45–48, 51–52, 76, 124, 140
  corporate profitability and, 38–40
  effect of minimum wage on, 139–140
  efficiencies in, 45, 48, 62, 120
  factors hindering hiring, 61

full-time, 27–28, 61, 80, 82, 132
geography and, 69–70
globalization effects on, 111
lifestyle and, 132–134, 154–155
lower opportunities for, 82–84
part-time, 27, 129
qualifications and requirements for, 72–73, 91
rates of, 93
temporary, 62
See also jobs
employment, benefits
health insurance, 58–61, 63, 128–130, 142
paid, excluding health, 65–66, 93
reduction of, 63–64, 65–66
employment, increasing
governmental policy, 100–102, 125–126, 127–128, 138–139, 139–140
tailoring education for, 103–105
employment status, 33f, 37f
under age of 15, 31
American expatriates, 31, 35–36
attending school/training, 30, 35
demand for jobs and, 34–36
discouraged workers, 30, 34
family responsibilities, 30, 35
ill health/disabilities, 30, 35
labor market and, 37, 40, 118, 121, 336
non-civilian/institutional, 31, 35–36
not seeking employment, 30–31, 35
retired, 67, 68–69
solidly employed, 29
unavailable to work, 30, 35

underemployed, 27–29
unemployed, 23–27
employment status movement, models of, 38f, 39f
The End of Work (Rifkin), 43
ENIAC (IBM), 19, 43, 49
entrepreneurship, 122, 123, 128
entry-level jobs, 83, 87, 104
Esposito, Dawn, 143
Evans, Christopher, 140
excess capacity of employees, 34, 76, 77, 104
exports and imports, 73–75, 109–110, 111, 113–114

Facebook, 47
family responsibilities, 30, 35
Fannie Mae, 113
Farm Security and Rural Investment Act (2002), 137
farm subsidies, 135–138, 142, 154
federal health care law (2010), 61, 129, 131
federal minimum wage, 100, 139–140, 142
Federal Reserve Bank, 69, 120
Ferguson, Niall, 112, 113
financial considerations and retirement, 67–69
Financial Times, 109
Finland, 130
Fisker, Jacob Lund, 133
Fitzpatrick, Robert L., 106
Forbes, 99
Ford, Martin, 46, 47, 57, 76, 77, 114, 131, 138, 141, 144, 159
foreign trade, 108–109, 111, 113
foreign workers, 74–75, 85, 117–120
See also immigration
Foroohar, Rana, 70, 75, 103
Fox, Vicente, 119
France, 92, 130, 134
Frankl, Viktor, 153
Freddie Mac, 113

free-trade zones, 109
Freud, Sigmund, 159
Friedman, George, 115
Friedman, Milton, 145
Friedman, Thomas, 47, 73, 75, 104
full adulthood
    dependent living
        arrangements, 81
    employment opportunities, 82–84
    and future job-market
        demand, 84–85
    marital age, 80–81
full-time employment, 27–28, 61, 80, 82, 132
fuzzy logic, 51

Galbraith, James K., 99
Galbraith, John Kenneth, 145
Gallup poll, 156
ganja, 92
Gates, Bill, 120
General Motors Corporation, 65, 129, 140
geography and employment, 69–70
Germany/Germans, 39, 73, 130, 141, 150
G.I. Bill, 18, 79
globalization, 21–22, 73, 74–76, 113
Goldman Sachs, 114
Google, 56
Gorz, Andre, 15, 154
governmental policy on increasing
    employment, 100–102, 125–126, 127–128, 138–139, 139–140, 142
governmental policy on subsidies, 135–138
government debt/spending, 100, 125–126
GPS devices, 51
Grassley, Charles, Sen., 137

Great Depression, 17, 96, 134
Great Recession, 22, 38, 70, 83, 88, 97
The Great Stagnation (Cowen), 18
Greece, 123, 130
Gross, Daniel, 66
gross domestic product (GDP), 59, 60, 110–111, 114, 130, 148
gross national product (GNP), 73, 148
growth rate in China, 111, 114
guaranteed income
    discussion, 143–146, 150–151, 160
    implementation, 149–150
    need for, 145, 147–149

Harford, Tim, 109
Harwood, John, 125
Haveman, Robert, 138
health care management (HMOs), 59–60, 158
health considerations and
    retirement, 67, 68–69
health effects of unemployment, 94, 98
health insurance
    early history of, 58, 59–61, 63
    governmental, 59, 86, 100, 130, 150
    private, 58–61, 63, 128–131
    separating from employment, 128–132, 142
health profile of Americans, 130, 157, 160
Heilbroner, Robert, 144
Henig, Robin Marantz, 84
Herbert, Bob, 17, 39–40, 91, 127
Heritage Foundation, 136
Herrnstein, Richard J., 145, 156
high unemployment and long-
    term unemployment, 90–91
hiring, trends in, 71–73
HIS Global Insight, 125

household income, 21, 63
housing and housing prices, 67, 68, 70, 82, 88, 126, 127, 133, 134
Houston (Texas), 34
Hufbauer, Gary C., 75
Huyck and Sons, 58

Iacocca, Lee, 129
ill health/disabilities, 30, 35
Imhoff, Daniel, 137
immigration
    competition with American workers, 119
    discussion, 117–118
    education levels of immigrants, 117, 118
    encouraged/non-restrictive, 120–121
    removing foreign workers, 74–75, 85, 117–120
    See also foreign workers
imports and exports, 73–75, 109–110, 111, 113–114
incentives to work, 150, 155
income-leveling activity, 150
income redistribution, 145, 147
independence indicators, 81–84
India, 21, 75, 85, 104, 111
Indonesia, 112
industrial productivity, 54
Industrial Revolution, 17, 54, 140, 150, 155
infant death rate, 130
inflation and inflation adjustments, 20, 59–60, 64, 65, 93
Information Age, 151
Infosys (India), 75
infrastructure, 100, 127–128, 132
institutional population, 31, 35–36
Intel, 56
Internal Revenue Service, 58
International Labour Office, 27

International Monetary Fund (IMF), 74–75
international trade, 108–109, 111, 113
Internet, 19, 111, 124, 154
involuntary part-time employment, 27
involuntary retirement, 87–89
Ireland, 123, 130
Italy, 123, 130
Ithaca Hours, 157

Jacques, Martin, 103, 112–113, 114, 115
Jamaica, 91–92
James, Bill, 89
Japan/Japanese, 73, 111, 112, 115, 120, 130
job creation/maintaining, 121, 123–124, 125, 127–128, 138–139
job force *See* labor force
job growth, 20
joblessness, 24, 44, 70, 79, 92, 96, 104, 143
    See also unemployment
job lock, 70, 128
job loss
    business and economic effects, 94
    in China, 114
    effects on crime, 95
    social effects of, 79, 91, 93–94, 96–97, 98
job replacement
    automation, 45–48, 124
    competition from foreign workers, 119
    globalization, 74–76, 112
    technology, 45–48, 50–51, 140
jobs
    advertising for, 71–73
    demand for, 32–34, 35–36, 75, 76

effect of minimum wage on,
    139–140
growth *vs.* loss, 20–23
non-governmental, 20, 38
types, classes of, 75–76
    See also employment
job sharing, 100, 141
Johnson, Lyndon B., 43–44, 145

Kahn, Herman, 147, 150
Kane, Tim, 121
Karabell, Zachary, 91, 112, 113,
    115
Keynes, John Maynard, 100, 160
Kilman, Scott, 137
King, Martin Luther, Jr., 161
Klein, Ezra, 128
Kocherlakota, Narayana, 69
Komarovsky, Mirra, 96
Korea/Koreans, 40, 46, 112
401k plans, 63–64, 65, 66
Krikorian, Mark, 120, 121
Krugman, Paul, 21, 45, 70, 90,
    91, 104
Kurzweil, Ray, 52

labor and scalability, 52–54
labor force
    advanced age of employees,
        67, 68–69
    delayed adulthood in, 82–85
    excess capacity of, 34, 76, 77,
        104
    mismatch of, 28–29, 69, 120
    participation of immigrants in,
        117–118, 120
    participation rates of, 20*f*, 83,
        95*f*
    size of, 47
    women in, 20, 38, 48, 82–83,
        97
labor market, 34–37, 40, 63–64,
    69–70, 80, 118, 121
labor scalability (relation to
    output), 52–56

laissez-faire capitalism, 160
Lampman, Robert, 145
latent demand for jobs, 32–34,
    36, 37
Latham, Tom, Rep., 137
Lawrence, Robert, 45
layoffs, 76, 87, 89
lean production, 62, 80
length of unemployment, 23–27,
    67, 86, 90–91, 94, 97, 132
Lerner theorem, 109
Let Them In (Riley), 119–120
Levy, Frank, 48
life expectancy/life span/longevity,
    68–69, 80, 98, 153, 160
life insurance, 65
lifestyle and employment, 132–
    134, 154–155, 160
The Lights in the Tunnel (Ford), 46
Loman, Willy (fictitious
    character), 154
London International Financial
    Futures and Options
    Exchange, 48
Luddite Fallacy, 57
Luttwak, Edward, 159
Luxembourg, 123

Macroeconomic Advisors, 125
MAD magazine, 44
managed care, 59
manual/non-repetitive jobs, 75
manufacturing jobs, 44, 45, 46,
    74, 76, 112, 120
Manulife Financial, 136
Mao Zedong, 21, 22, 110
marriage and marital age, 80–81,
    96, 97
Mary Kay products, 122
McArdle, Megan, 72, 104
McDonalds, 56
McIntyre, Douglas A., 99
MeadWestvaco, 136
mean/median income, 147
mechanization, 45, 46, 50, 52,
    147

Medicare, 59, 86, 89, 100, 102, 131
medium of exchange, 157–158
men
  full adulthood, 80–81, 83
  joblessness and, 93, 94, 97, 98, 119
merging economies, 112–113
Mexico/Mexicans, 74, 118, 119, 120, 121, 134
Meyerson, Harold, 43
Miami Time Dollar network, 157
Microsoft, 54, 55, 56, 57, 62, 120
Miller, Arthur, 154
Milwaukee (Wisconsin), 85, 92, 93
minimum wage (federal), 100, 138–140, 142
60 Minutes (CBS), 106
Miron, Jeffrey A., 99
mismatch of labor force, 28–29, 69, 120
Moody's Economy.com, 125
"mossbacks," 86
Moynihan, Daniel Patrick, 149
multilevel marketing (MLM), 105–107
Murnane, Richard J., 48
Murray, Charles, 145, 156
mutual funds, 45

National Commission on Guaranteed Incomes, 145
National Federation of Independent Business, 70
National Football League, 89
National Intelligence Council, 114
National Research Council, 118
national wage insurance system, 100
native-born Americans, 118–119, 121
naturalized citizens, 117
Netherlands, 130
"network outsourcing," 74

new business, 121, 123–124
New Jobs Tax Credit, 138
Newman, Rick, 34, 67–68, 97, 99
New Passages (Sheehy), 80
Newsweek, 70, 138, 154
Newton, Isaac, 160
New York (state), 157
New York Families and Work Institute, 88
The New York Times, 39, 99, 125
New Zealand, 123, 134
non-algorithmic skills, 50
non-civilian population, 31, 35–36
nongovernmental organizations *See* charitable/non-profit organizations
non-native workers, 74–75, 85, 117–120
not seeking employment, 30–31, 35
Nutrilite, 106

Obama, Barack, 77, 103, 127, 138
oil, 20, 115
Okun's Law, 64
older workers, 85–89
omnibus legislation, 135
online classified ads, 71–72
Orlando (Florida), 71, 72, 85
Orrenius, Pia, 120
Ose, Doug, Rep., 137
outsourcing, 45, 74–75, 85, 96, 104

Paine, Thomas, 144, 145
Panama, 134
part-time employment, 27, 129
Paulson, Henry M., 74
Peace Corps, 144, 146
Peck, Don, 79, 80, 97, 98
pension plans, 63–64, 65
Perot, Ross, 74
personal leave, paid, 66
Peter, Laurence J., 86

Pew Hispanic Foundation, 119
Philadelphia (Pennsylvania), 93
Pippen, Scottie, 137
Player Piano (Vonnegut), 51, 150
Portland (Oregon), 157
Portugal, 123, 134
post-industrial productivity, 54–56
poverty, 89, 111, 144, 154
preferred provider organizations
    (PPOs), 59–60
pre-industrial productivity, 52–53
prices
    automation effects on, 47
    consumer, 138, 142, 153
    globalization effects on, 73–75
primary work, 147, 149*f*
Producers Rice Mill, 136
productivity
    automation effects on, 47–48,
        51
    industrial period, 54
    post-industrial period, 54–56
    pre-industrial period, 52–53
    relation to jobs, 64–65,
        140–141
professional jobs, 75, 96, 120
Project Management Institute.
    Central Florida Chapter, 72
protectionism, 107–110, 113, 137
public policy, 104
public works/infrastructure, 100,
    127–128, 132
Putnam, Robert P., 98, 157
pyramid schemes, 106

qualifications and requirements for
    employment, 72–73, 91
quantitative easing, 126
quaternary work, 147–148
Quigley, William P., 138, 139, 144

Rastafarians, 91–92, 94
rates and length of unemployment,
    23–27, 67, 71, 86, 90–91, 94,
    97, 132, 139

recession (2008-2009), 68–69,
    114, 123, 132
recessions, 21–23, 43, 62, 74, 81
Reich, Robert B., 99
religion and lifestyle, 133
relocation, 85, 96, 119, 134
replacement of workers, 45–48,
    74–76, 112, 119, 124
resources, using, 110
résumés, 91, 104
retirement
    financial considerations,
        67–69
    involuntary, 87–89
    plans and pensions, 63–64,
        65, 87–88
    relocation, 134
retraining employees, 100, 103–
    105
reverse brain drain, 95–96
Reynolds, Joyce K., 106
rice, 136
Riceland Foods, 136
Rifkin, Jeremy, 43, 45, 46, 76, 91,
    128, 141, 143, 144, 151, 155,
    158, 159
Riley, Jason L., 119–120
robots/robotics, 44, 45, 46, 49,
    50, 62, 75, 120, 121
Rodgers, T.J., 120
Room for Debate (blog), 99
Roosevelt, Franklin D., 135, 144
Rosin, Hanna, 97
Russell, Bertrand, 145
Russia, 40, 95

Saint-Simon, Paul de, 145
sales jobs, 124–125
sales per employee, 56, 76
Samsung, 107
Samuelson, Robert J., 38, 39, 70,
    72, 90, 99, 123, 125, 137
Sauter, Michael B., 99
savings and savings rate, 67, 88,
    112

scalability
    automation and, 56–57
    business sales per employee, 56
    labor related to output, 52–56
scaling up, 74
Schell, Jim, 117, 122
Scientific American, 43
Scott, Robert, 112, 127
secondary work, 147, 148, 149*f*
self-employed workers, 89, 123,
    124, 128
service jobs, 44, 45, 74, 147,
    148–149
shadow wage, 143–144
Shane, Scott, 128
Sheehy, Gail, 80, 82
shortening the workweek, 140–
    141, 142
sick leave, paid, 65
Singapore, 114
the Singularity, 52
skills
    algorithmic/non-algorithmic,
        49, 50
    effect of long-term
        unemployment on, 90–91
    employment status and, 27–
        29, 30, 76–77
    of foreign workers/immigrants,
        117
    structural unemployment and,
        69
    wages and, 47
small business, 100, 105, 121–124
Small Business for Dummies (Tyson
    and Schell), 122
Sneeding, Timothy, 131
social capital, 155–157
Social Security, 67, 88, 100, 118
Social Security Administration,
    87, 118
Social Security disability, 32
social wage, 144, 145
software, 45, 46, 47
solidly employed, 29

Sørenson, Aage B., 80
South Korea, 46, 73
soybeans, 136
Spain, 123, 130
standard retirement age, 67, 68
start-up business, 121, 123–124
Steingart, Gabor, 94, 113, 160
Stevenson, Betsey, 70, 103, 141
structural unemployment, 69–71
Summers, Larry, 123, 125
Sumner, Daniel, 137
"survival jobs," 77
Switzerland, 112, 130

Target, 32
tax cuts and remedies, 100, 101,
    102, 138–139, 142
technology
    changes in, 90–91
    job replacement, 44–46,
        50–51, 140
    post-industrial, 55–56
    types of, 40, 52, 71, 75
tertiary work, 147, 148, 149*f*
Thailand, 73, 112, 134
The Atlantic, 79, 97, 99
Theobald, Robert, 144, 145
The World is Flat (Friedman), 73
Thoma, Mark, 99
Thompson, Derek, 99, 112
Thurow, Roger, 137
Tobin, James, 145
Toffler, Alvin, 140
Toles, Tom, 38–39
Toshiba, 107
Townsend, Peter, 88
Townsend, Robert, 86
trade tariffs and quotas, 108–109,
    110, 137
treasury bonds (U.S.), 112, 113
Turner, Ted, 137
Twitter, 47
Tyson, Eric, 117, 122

unavailable to work, 30, 35

underclass, non-working or
permanent, 91, 93–94
underemployment, 27–29
unemployment
among young black males, 94
in China, 114
demand for jobs and, 34,
63–64, 69
health effects of, 94, 98
insurance benefits, 100, 128,
132, 141
levels of, 20–21, 38–40
of older workers, 67, 68–69,
86–87
prison populations, 94–95
productivity and, 64–65
rates and length of, 23–27,
67, 71, 86, 90–91, 94, 97,
132, 139
structural, 69–71
See also joblessness
unions, 65, 90, 101, 140
United Arab Emirates, 65
United Auto Workers (UAW), 65
United Kingdom/Great Britain/
Britons, 130, 131, 145
United States, 111, 130
United States. Bureau of Labor
Statistics (BLS), 23, 27, 30,
32, 68
United States. Census Bureau, 23,
31
United States. Centers for Disease
Control, 69
United States. Congressional
Budget Office, 125
United States. Department of
Labor, 23, 70, 103
United States. House of
Representatives, 112
universal health care
(governmental), 150
unskilled workers, 47
"untouchables," 75
Urban Poverty and Family Life

Study (Chicago), 94
U.S. News & World Report, 34,
38, 99
vacations, paid, 65
Value Added Tax (VAT), 149
Vietnam, 112, 134
virtual jobs, 144
visas, H-1B, 120
vocational training, 104
Volunteers in Service to America
(VISTA), 144
volunteer work, 143, 144, 156–
157, 158
Vonnegut, Kurt, Jr., 51, 150

Wage and Hour Act, 140
wages
automation effect on, 47–48
education and, 118–119
effects of job loss on, 93
federal minimum wage, 100,
138–140, 142
globalization effect on, 74–75
immigration effects on, 118–
119, 120
layoff effects on, 87
national wage insurance, 100
productivity and, 64–65
unskilled workers, 47
24/7 Wall St., 99
The Wall Street Journal, 119, 137
Wal-Mart, 32, 56, 111, 138
The Washington Post, 38–39, 99,
137
W.E. Upjohn Institute, 138
Wellesley College, 87
What Color Is Your Parachute?
(Bolles), 29
wheat, 136
white-collar jobs, 75, 96, 120
White House Council of
Economic Advisors, 70, 125
Wiener, Norbert, 44
Wilson, William Julius, 79, 93,
95, 128

Winning By Default Years, 18, 63, 73, 79, 81
Wolgemuth, Liz, 103
women
    full adulthood, 81–82
    joblessness, 92, 96
    as part of labor force, 20, 38, 48, 82–83, 97
work
    consumption and, 57, 58
    economic subdivisions of, 147–149
    incentives to, 150, 155
    See also employment
workers *See* employees
working hours per week, 27–29, 63, 93, 130–131, 140–141, 142
work responsibilities, changes in, 47–48
Work's New Age, discussion of, 15, 17–23, 159–161
Work's New Age, Principles of
    concerning age of workers, 69, 81
    concerning automation and scalability, 46, 56
    concerning consumers and consumption, 107, 147, 148
    concerning job loss and unemployment, 39, 63, 76, 109, 124, 148
    other, 71, 129
"work society," 159
Works Progress Administration (WPA), 100, 127–128, 142, 144
World War I, 17
World War II, 18, 40, 58, 79, 135
World Wide Web, 21
Wu, Mark, 112

Yard, Margaret, 143
Yom Kippur War, 19–20
younger workers, 83

yuan renminbi, 112, 113–114

Zakaria, Fareed, 112, 113, 115, 126
Zandi, Mark, 125, 132
Zuckerman, Mortimer P., 38, 46, 69, 70, 99, 103, 120, 147

About the Author

James B. Huntington has been a business professor, teacher, and professional speaker. His 2007 doctoral dissertation is the only book written on career jobs for post-65 baby boomers. He has also written scholarly works on leadership, organizational change, and human development.

FAST ORDER FORM

Fax orders:
   845-557-0353. Use this form.
Telephone orders, by credit card or PayPal:
   845-456-0115.
Email orders:
   Send to orders@royalflushpress.com.
Mail orders:
   Royal Flush Press, P.O. Box 190, Eldred, NY 12732

Please send _____copy (or copies) of *Work's New Age*, for
   US $17.95 apiece, to:

Name: _____

Address: _____

   _____

City_____

State _____ ZIP Code _____

Telephone _____

Email address: _____

___ Cash or check (enclosed)

___ MasterCard, Visa, or Discover: Card number and
   expiration date: _____

___ PayPal: Use email address above,
   or _____ .

Sales tax: Please add 6% for delivery to New York State.

Shipping for *entire order* (no extra charge for more than
   one book):

   U.S. Media Mail $2.00,
   U.S. Priority Mail $5.00,
   Foreign Priority Mail $12.00

FAST ORDER FORM

Fax orders:
    845-557-0353. Use this form.
Telephone orders, by credit card or PayPal:
    845-456-0115.
Email orders:
    Send to orders@royalflushpress.com.
Mail orders:
    Royal Flush Press, P.O. Box 190, Eldred, NY 12732

Please send _____copy (or copies) of *Work's New Age*, for
    US $17.95 apiece, to:
Name: _____
Address: _____

        _____
City_____
State _____ ZIP Code _____
Telephone _____
Email address: _____
____ Cash or check (enclosed)
____ MasterCard, Visa, or Discover: Card number and
        expiration date: _____
____ PayPal: Use email address above,
        or _____ .

Sales tax: Please add 6% for delivery to New York State.
Shipping for *entire order* (no extra charge for more than
    one book):

    U.S. Media Mail $2.00,
    U.S. Priority Mail $5.00,
    Foreign Priority Mail $12.00

FAST ORDER FORM

Fax orders:
    845-557-0353. Use this form.

Telephone orders, by credit card or PayPal:
    845-456-0115.

Email orders:
    Send to orders@royalflushpress.com.

Mail orders:
    Royal Flush Press, P.O. Box 190, Eldred, NY 12732

Please send _____copy (or copies) of *Work's New Age*, for US $17.95 apiece, to:

Name: _____

Address: _____

    _____

City_____

State _____ ZIP Code _____

Telephone _____

Email address: _____

___ Cash or check (enclosed)

___ MasterCard, Visa, or Discover: Card number and
    expiration date: _____

___ PayPal: Use email address above,
    or _____ .

Sales tax: Please add 6% for delivery to New York State.

Shipping for *entire order* (no extra charge for more than one book):

    U.S. Media Mail $2.00,
    U.S. Priority Mail $5.00,
    Foreign Priority Mail $12.00